A Man And His Mission

AN AUTOBIOGRAPHY BY CLAUDE A. GUILD

A TEXT ON MISSIONARY METHODS

ISBN 0-940999-53-6

Published By

Bible Publications, Inc.
Fort Worth, Texas 76182

Dedicated to
my grandchildren and great-grandchildren:

Mark, Jon, Douglas, Hugh, Chris, Heather, Eric,
Theron, Eliot, Jade, Tina, Zachary and Joshua

CONTENTS

PREFACE

As David "served the will of God in his generation" (Acts 13:36), so Claude and Sammie Guild, from their youth, like Ezra, "set" their "heart to seek the law of Jehovah, and to do it, and to teach" (Ezra 7:10) it to all who would hear.

God can only use as vessels of honor people so minded and so dedicated. Heaven will have thousands of souls who would not have arrived had it not been for the unselfish love in the hearts of Claude and Sammie for their Savior and for all mankind. In addition to eternal life, Claude and Sammie "will receive a reward" (yes, there are degrees of joy in heaven, I Corinthians 3:14). Part of the happiness of Claude and Sammie in that land fairer than day will be in their being reunited forever with souls they caused to turn from darkness to light (cf. Acts 26:18). Part of Paul's extra heavenly happiness he believed would be to see again and forever the Thessalonians whom he had converted: "What is our hope or joy or crown of exultation before our Lord Jesus at his coming? Is it not you? You are our glory and joy" (I Thessalonians 2:19-20).

A personal thrill to me, since I have been a long-time admirer of this Christian couple, has been the privilege of reading the beautiful story of their lives in this matchless book even before its printing. I am enriched by the reading, and may thousands of people have the same happy experience.

Hugo McCord

i

INTRODUCTION

It is with pleasure that I write the introduction to my father's account of his life story. It is a story bound up in his calling — his mission to preach the gospel. As I reflect on my own remembrances of his life, they, too, are embedded in his mission.

As I recall the past and my memories of Daddy, I remember him most as a gospel preacher. Even my memories of him as a father are shaped and colored by my vision of him as a preacher. I have always been proud to be a preacher's daughter, and his influence on my life has been profound. His love for the Word and the church has enriched my life and provided me a sense of my own mission. I believe he has even influenced my own style of public speaking as I fulfill my calling to teach the Word.

He preaches with enthusiasm, emotion and passion. He often refers to his enthusiastic pulpit manner as "windmill" preaching. Those who have heard him preach certainly know what he means. His enthusiasm always created an interest in me as I listened to his sermons.

He also preaches with great ranges of emotion. I have always loved his humor, although I have often been embarrassed by it — especially when I was a child and the object of his illustration. But he allows himself to be vulnerable. He is real. He relates personal stories and risks exposure. He allows his own message to touch his heart and move him to tears — as a result his audiences are moved.

His preaching is more than emotion and enthusiasm. He is motivated by his passion for lost souls, the gospel, and the people of God. He deeply loves his God and the church for which He died. This passion is what informs his calling and compels him to pursue his mission.

I fondly remember many of his sermons. He is a master of imagery and creates vivid impressions that I have carried a lifetime. Often his images are suggested in his titles. The most cleaver and humorous that I remember is his sermon on the prodigal son, "How to Give a Pig a Permanent Wave." I recall his sermon on the establishment of the church and the charts he used to take the "rabbit through the log." However, the most vivid memory I have is of a sermon I heard when I was about ten years old that started my own journey of faith. It was on the ten virgins and entitled, "Just Outside the Door." I marvel that I can remember these so well, along with others, but that is a tribute to his preaching.

I also remember great preaching services with what seemed as standing room only. That is what I recall of the Sunday morning I was baptized. The aisle down which I walked was lined with people who had been sitting in folding chairs brought in to accommodate the crowd. Those services at the Riverside church and what I remember as baptisms every Sunday, were great days for me at a very impressionable age.

I also remember Sunday worship services and gospel meetings when we sang "Just as I am" over and over because people continued to come forward. And we all thrilled to the stories of people who were brought to Christ as he returned from his gospel meetings.

As I read these pages I was struck by how much he was away from home. Yet I do not remember his being gone so much. I am puzzled by why that is, but I have concluded it is because of a steady and faithful mother who kept us secure while he was away. Mother also provided the support and security he needed through the hardships of laboring in distant and difficult fields. She is the model I have looked to as I have labored beside my own husband. Theirs is an unshakable marriage and truly a gift to their children.

Daddy has always had a wonderful gift of remembering people's names. There are so many names in this book, as he recounts the conversions of individuals and families and recalls the support of people around the world who shared in his mission. He also documents the beginnings of numerous congregations. Therefore, this is more than his story. It is also the story of the church in many places, but especially in the Pacific Northwest where his mission began.

This past April, Mother and Daddy were honored at the Pepperdine University Lectureship for their lifetime of Christian service. Dr. Jerry Rushford made a statement when he presented them with their plaque, "Claude and Sammie have had a map of the world etched on their hearts."

It has been a remarkable experience to read and edit this book. It stirred up memories, revealed things I did not know, and gave me a greater sense of Daddy's calling. I am most thankful I have had this opportunity to help him tell his story.

D'Esta Lea Love

Chapter 1

THE FAMILY SETTING

Charles Attlee Guild, my father, was born in Des Moines, Iowa, November 29, 1882. My grandfather, Charles A. Guild, was engaged in nursery work and farming. He owned a 260 acre farm in Webster County, Iowa, and there he farmed and raised high grade cattle. Together with my grandmother, Tommy Guild, they raised a family of ten children, the oldest of which was a son, Clarence. My father was the second child born into the family.

An early incident which became legendary in my family history occurred when my father was a very young man. A neighborhood feud developed between the Guilds and a neighboring family, the Bickers, over a fence line. One day my grandfather, along with Clarence and my father, was building a fence inside the disputed line when the Bricker brothers rode up on horseback and shot and killed my grandfather, Charles A. Guild, and my uncle, Clarence. The Bricker brothers were given ninety-nine years for their crimes.

Charles A. Guild was an honest and good man. Like his father before him, he was a Republican and a member of the Woodmen of the World. He and his oldest son, Clarence, were laid to rest in the Oakwood Cemetery, Stratford, Iowa.

Following the murder of my grandfather, it became the responsibility of my grandmother and my father to raise the family and manage the farm. Tommy Guild had a degree from Huntsville Female College and was a lady of culture and refinement. She and Charles Attlee managed the family affairs and farmed together until 1911 when Charles reached twenty -seven years.

In 1911, Charles Attlee Guild met and married Ella Otelia Olsen of Hayward, Minnesota. They farmed four years in Iowa and then joined other neighbors to homestead in Montana in 1915. They settled in Fergus county, with Lewiston as the county seat, and they lived six miles west of the township of Buffalo. There they raised cattle, grain and opened a coal mine in Coal Mine Canyon. There were born to them ten children: four boys and six girls (Charles Seivart, Neaoma Andrena, Claude Adrian, Robert Franklin, Mary Ellen, Grace Blanche, Ruth Esther, Dorothy Louise, Audrey Louella Roselea and George Edward).

Most adults reflect on their childhood and many try to recall the very first thing they can remember. I have recited my first memory many, many times. I was between two and three years of age. Uncle Chris Olson, a brother of my grandfather, had come to visit from Chicago, Illinois. After a two-week visit he was to meet the train in Buffalo the next day; therefore, the family planned the activities for the next day, prior to his leaving. My father announced that he was going to dig a new toilet hole and move the toilet in the morning before Uncle Chris' departure. It was a two holer, and that night I stayed awake wondering how Dad would take on such a big job. Early the next morning I watched through the window as Daddy and Uncle Chris dug the new hole. After lunch, my mother told me if I would take my nap I could go with Daddy and Uncle Chris to the train in the buggy. But, the activities outside were too exciting to nap. I watched as they took the wagon box off the running gears. Daddy backed the wheels up to the toilet, then he and Uncle Chris laid it on the running gears, took it to the new hole and set it upright. About that time Mother came in the room, warmed my britches for not napping and ruled out going to Buffalo to see Uncle Chris off on the train. Nevertheless, I

2

always believed the sacrifice of a nap was worth the whipping and forfeiting the trip and other goodies just to see that big construction job completed.

My next memories were common occurrences but remarkable for a young boy. We would be put to bed and although the bedroom door would be open and a reflection of the wood fire would be seen, more vivid sights appeared outside. It was not uncommon on many nights to see wolves and coyotes looking in our bedroom windows. This would frighten most children, but we were used to them. Many times as we travelled in the wagon the family dog would chase coyotes into the timberline and return crying for his life with wolves on his tail, and he would jump in the wagon to escape them.

Another highlight of my youth was the Singer sewing machine salesman's annual visit. He had an extra big wagon, carried a dozen or more sewing machines, drove four head of horses, two abreast, and made our place his home as he visited the other ranchers. Mother and Daddy mentioned one day that it was time for him to come and wondered if he was doing all right with his artificial leg. This subject created a lot of interest on our part, but we were warned not to say anything about it when he came. He arrived with his usual pomp and sales conversations. After supper, he oiled mother's old peddle machine and sat by the fire visiting with the family. Then the moment for which we were all waiting arrived. He crossed his legs and as he began to swing his top leg it began to squeak. Neaoma jumped up, ran through the dining room to Mother and said, "Now I know which leg it is!". It was too bad the old boy oiled the sewing machine and forgot a few drops of oil on the hinge of his wooden leg.

We never lacked things to do and activities to keep our interest. My father held state titles in Iowa in wrestling and boxing. When he opened his coal mine, miners from many parts of the nation came to work. We had some who

3

were AWOL with the army, some who were on dope, others who liked liquor. After supper there wasn't much to do, and Dad would bring out the boxing gloves, especially for newcomers. During twelve years of mining and boxing, many challengers came and went but never did a miner deck Charlie Guild.

We had many other encounters with miners through the years. Mr. Stalk was a good miner, but he was on dope so Daddy had to fire him. After two weeks passed, he phoned from town claiming that Dad owed him $80.00 and he was coming out to get the money. Daddy knew he was paid in full, but he also knew Stalk was out of funds and wanted dope. Stalk threatened to come after the $80.00 and shoot Dad if he did not get it. Daddy immediately made plans to handle the situation. He saddled his best roan horse, kissed Mother good-bye and rode for the sheriff. The sheriff overtook Mr. Stalk; he was jailed, tried and never again allowed back in Fergus county. Another young miner was like a homesick boy. Mother would have him up to the ranch for supper often. Just before an evening meal one winter night, military police arrived and arrested the young miner for being absent without leave. They wanted to take him immediately. Mother came forward and begged the officers not to take him until after he ate. They consented and Mother was relieved.

A crisis in our family history occurred shortly after the birth of the sixth child, Grace Blanche, March 16, 1925. My mother suffered a long illness because of a pulmonary embolism in her left lung, which necessitated an extended stay in the hospital. There were no medicines such as penicillin, and seven different doctors gave her little hope to survive. This long illness and the resulting hospital confinement caused her to read her Bible to find answers to questions she had about her own spiritual welfare, as well as that of her children left on the homestead. She spent long

4

hours reading her Bible, and when she wasn't able to read, Daddy read to her.

Mother was raised a Lutheran, and, about the time of their marriage, Daddy embraced the Lutheran faith also. Neither one of them had been immersed for baptism and this was troubling to them. They also struggled with the doctrine of the original sin, or the curse of Adam's sin on each individual born into this world. The Lutheran minister was called on numerous occasions for confession as she had been taught in the Catechism. "Confession consists of two parts: the one is, that we confess our sins; the other, that we receive absolution or forgiveness through the pastor as of God himself, in no wise doubting, but firmly believing that our sins are thus forgiven before God in heaven." (L.S.C. p. 79) My parents had just read in their Bibles, "And if any man sin, we have an Advocate with the Father (not the pastor) Jesus Christ the righteous." (I John 2:1) They asked the pastor about this and immersion for baptism, and he told them on more than one occasion that if they didn't quit reading the Bible my mother would go crazy. Well, it was difficult to have seven doctors tell you that you can't live, but to have your pastor say you would go crazy too only added to the complications.

During this trying time for Mother and Daddy, it would be of great interest to learn how the five older children were managing on the ranch. We were normal children and had strong desires to try some things we hadn't done with our parents at home. For example, there was a large trunk in the attic that had always been a temptation to open. When our parents were at home this was an "off limits" activity. One long Saturday afternoon we got the urge to pull the trunk down and see what it held. We found, to our surprise, clothes we had owned when we were little, medium and larger. I was overjoyed to find a sailor's suit I had owned years before, and, since Bob and I couldn't get ours on, we knew we had grown a lot. There were other family treasures in the trunk like mother's wedding dress, lots of gifts in jewelry and keepsakes. After our delightful afternoon of discovery, everything was put away and the trunk returned to its original place.

It was spring time and the hens were laying lots of eggs, but no one was at home to take them to the store and trade them for groceries. We gathered them and put them in safe keeping. When Dad returned, to his surprise he found a six weeks' supply of eggs stored in shoe boxes, a ten gallon cream can and even burlap bags. To his greater surprise, all the eggs were good, and the grocer was glad to trade them.

Charles and I were instructed to go to the coal mine on Saturdays and load wagons that would come for coal, since miners had Saturdays off. (The miners had filled a chute that would perhaps hold thirty tons of coal.) We rode horses to the mine and waited for wagons to come. We had often seen miners roll their own cigarettes and smoke. So while we waited, we went into the shacks, found some Bull Durham tobacco, filled papers, rolled and licked them, and in spite of a few lumps in the cigarettes, they smoked pretty good. Charles thought with the lumps in them they looked like camels with humps (he had heard of that brand of tailor-made cigarettes but never used them.) As a consequence of our big time smoking experience, we both got so dizzy we could hardly ride our horses to the ranch house that evening.

Long days at the ranch were lonesome without parents and the usual assigned activities. We recalled hearing the train whistle three times a week as it rolled through the Twin Sisters Mountains to the east of the ranch. We often wondered what it would be like to ride on that train. Some of the smaller children had not even seen it. If they had, they might have felt just like the Arkansas family that drove to town to see the train come through. When the family returned home, the mother asked the daddy and the

6

boys what the train was like. The old gentleman said, "Ma, you wouldn't believe it. That train came into town endwise but it was so long, if it had come in sideways, it would have wiped the whole town out."

Visitors to the ranch were far and few between. One visitor was a joy to the children. He was an Indian we all called Hank. He would work with threshing crews, help with the early plowing and put up hay. He dropped in on us and spent a day or two. He taught us how to make bows and arrows by using Willow wood. He cut grooves in the end of the arrows and had us raid the chicken house for feathers. He carefully stripped the feathers and tied them in a circular position in the grooves on the arrow. He then put a needle or nail in the point of the arrow. They were wonderful. They would spin as they flew through the air and they would stick in the side of the barn, a tree or the hind leg of a cow, as one did on one occasion. We had the place pretty well shot up when Dad returned on one of his visits.

Riding for the mail boxes was also great sport. The mail carrier had a large wheel on a post about a half mile from our school. Everyone's mail box was on the wheel. The children always knew when their parents would make out an order with Montgomery Ward for Christmas presents, because they asked the children to mail the order. Being children, they thought Montgomery Ward was just over the ridge and would fill the order the next day. Hence, there would be a race to the mail boxes every day to see if the package had come from the mail-order house. After three weeks of races for the box, there was a large package. Charles , since he was the oldest, got to carry it home. When we stopped to open the gates we would shake it and squeeze it and try to figure out what was in it. Mother took the delivery and where she hid it before Christmas still is a great mystery, but it would all be there and never was one child ever forgotten.

School was great at the Coal Mine School. We had eight grades in one room. Everyone came to school on horseback. In cold weather we were introduced to a tub of snow in the foyer of the building. We all removed our gloves, shoes and socks and washed our faces, hands and feet in the snow to remove frostbite. One of our teachers was single and the cowboys liked her. We had great fun making jokes about her — especially her name, which was hard to pronounce — Miss Henchitt (enough said). When the cowboys came during the day to court the teacher, she would ride off with them and leave Sybil Olson, one of our eighth-grade cousins, in charge of the classes. Little learning took place, but we had lots of fun.

The Coal Mine School had no planned play ground and no specific physical education program; therefore, we created our own. It was great sport in the spring to bring a cord string to school, place it carefully over a gopher hole, lie down in back of the hole, wait for one to stick his head up and snare him. We would run to the schoolhouse to "show and tell," and the teacher would kill the gopher to reduce their population. The best extracurricular activity, however, came when Indian Hank visited school and showed us an Indian cemetery within a half mile of the school. There never has been a sport as exciting as digging those graves. Hank showed us the difference between an Indian skull and white-man's skull. There were five bones in the Indian skull. (Skull seams of an Indian did not come to a point on top but to another bone about the size of a quarter, a bone caucasion skulls did not have.) We found pottery, corn grinders, arrowheads, dog bones, rugs and kept very little of it. We dug to find a white-man's skull but never found one.

While we managed on the farm as best we could, doing our chores, going to school and pursuing our great adventures, Mother and Daddy continued to read their Bible with great fervor. Finally she gained enough strength to go home, but she did not abandon her prayerful vigil for the truth. I recall her telling many, many times how she walked along the timber line and prayed, "Lord, send us the truth. We want to know your will." In a matter of months, word came on the community phone line through Cecil Barnhart, a rancher and neighbor, that there would be preaching at the Coal Mine school house. J.C. Bailey from Radville, Sask., Canada, was the young evangelist with a nondenominational message. It was in that school house where we first learned the difference between denominationalism and New Testament Christianity. Two people present at the meeting requested baptism by immersion: my mother and her sister-in-law, Mrs. Chris Olson.

Arrangements for the baptisms were made by using a triple-bed wagon box to dam the creek. While they waited for the water to rise, neighbors and family members rode their horses through the water to muddy it — to curse and threaten Bailey and frighten the two women. Mrs. Chris Olson was frightened and was not baptized, but Mother stepped forward and was baptized by immersion for the remission of sins. Bailey continued the meeting in the school house. Recognizing Daddy's need for more time to study the issues, Bailey took a job in the coal mine and taught him as he mined coal. Later Daddy was baptized, along with my older brother and sister, Charles and Neaoma. (All this occurred in the framework of about three months.)

We asked Bailey where we would go to church and who would be our pastor. (We leaned heavily on the pastors in the Lutheran church.) He informed us that there wasn't a congregation of the churches of Christ in Montana nor was there a minister or pastor. However, he volunteered to send us Sunday school lessons and taught Mother how to bake the communion bread in her own oven, so we could carry on in our own house. This we did, and Bro. J.C. Bailey was very faithful in sending the necessary lessons and admonitions we needed to stay alive in Christ.

9

After her baptism, Mother continued to improve, but she was still in need of care. It was decided that each of the four oldest children would stay home from school a week at a time to do the cooking and housekeeping. (This included chopping the wood, going to the spring for water, ringing the necks of chickens, making cornbread or a cake, peeling lots of potatoes and other vegetables and gathering watercress for salads. We also learned as many as six or eight ways to fix eggs.) Few would ever see value in this for three boys. However, I left for college in Texas in 1935 and batched with twenty-one other preacher boys. I knew how to make the best cornbread in the boarding house. Boys would line up with their meal, eggs and other mixings, and I would fix the batter. Only in later years did Betty Crocker out-bake my cornbread.

Cold winter days and nights in Montana had an influence on families, school and church. The snow would be six to eight feet deep and crust over. Families would use teams and sleds, with straw and blankets. They would carry poles to raise the telephone lines to get the teams and rigs under the wires. Horses would be cold and often threw the children as they opened gates on the way to school. One day the neighbors had a big Christmas party at Uncle Hermon Olson's. They took a group picture when it was sixty below zero. Uncle Johnny said it was really colder than that and he was sure of it. According to him, it was the lowest the thermometer read and even colder. It got so cold it bent the nail on the wall. (This became a long-standing family joke about the Montana weather.)

When I was ten-years-old, Mother had to go to Lewistown for a week for dental work. My parents farmed out all the children but me. Daddy was hauling grain and wanted me to drive a wheat wagon to the elevator in Buffalo. Driving four head of horses, two abreast, was a dream come true for a young boy. (Daddy knew there would be no problems because the rear wagon could do little but follow the ruts of the front wagon, but the rear driver would have to keep his team from eating out of the lead wagon.) We made it fine going to town but on the way home the wagons were empty and noisy. As we approached the homestead, I saw lights on at the house and I knew none of the family should be there. I lost my voice calling to my father but to no avail. Finally, we stopped to open the gate and then I could ask my father about the lights. Daddy said, "Oh, it's some cowboy that has come for the night." It was a long and anxious wait at the barn while the eight head of horses were unharnessed, curried, fed and bedded. We made our way to the house and, sure enough, there was Andy Carpenter, a leading rider in rodeos. He had peeled potatoes, fried some side meat and found the homemade bread. He was welcomed and everyone was at ease.

Fortunately, with peace of mind spiritually, Mother's health improved and the doctors thought she could completely recover if we moved to a lower elevation. The hospital and doctor's fees took most of the funds from the sale of the ranch and coal mine, and in late 1926, we moved to Wilder, Idaho. We were a family of six at that time. The depression came and the family pooled its funds to survive. Nevertheless, there was great joy in our hearts because we had moved near a church of Christ, 16th and Everett Sts., Caldwell, Idaho. The church had about twenty members, and they were glad to see a new and large family move into their midst. Mother and Daddy related their conversions, and in 1928 the Caldwell church invited J.C. Bailey for a revival meeting. It was during that meeting that my brother, Bob, and I obeyed the gospel. The baptisms were in the waters of the Boise River.

Mother prayed to live long enough to see all her children become Christians. This great lady and pioneer in the gospel for families of the Guild people not only lived but gave birth to four more children in Idaho. As time passed, her older children began to marry, and she took a new petition to the Father to live long enough to see all the in-laws of her family obey the gospel. It certainly wasn't unexpected that grandchildren and great-grandchildren would be born. Therefore, she made another major request in prayer that she could live to see the grandchildren obey the gospel. She lived eighty-three years. At her funeral service in Eugene, Oregon, the minister, Virgil Jackson, related how all her children, her in-laws but one and all her grand and great grandchildren, who were old enough, had obeyed the gospel. It made a total of forty-seven souls. "Let her works praise her in the gates." (Proverbs 31:31)

Idaho and the Depression

After owning the ranch and coal mines in Montana, Daddy, affectionately called Charlie by his friends, became a share cropper in Idaho. However, as a family we were aware of one fundamental fact — true wealth was in the treasures we had in Christ. This new relationship prepared us for the impending depression, and it found us moving from farm to farm and school to school. One year we farmed for Mr. Karnes in the Wilder community, then we moved to the Rockwood community. (Karnes was drilling for oil in Montana and was the person who encouraged our family to move to Idaho where the elevations would be less than half that in Montana and the climate less severe. The doctors concurred in the decision for mother's sake.) The Rock-wood farm gave us opportunity to recover some of our losses. One loss we regained was the piano, which tied the family together. Daddy knew how to play and had learned scores of great classics of his time and was a good singer. Some of the favorites I remember are: "Custer's last Stand," "We're Just Good Friends, your Mother and Me," "Ivan Skivincie Skivar," and many children's songs. They also bought a Buick touring car for transportation to church. In

12

addition, they saw all the children enrolled in the Wilder school.

Because of a school fire, my seventh-grade class had its school in an old lumberyard building. We found it an ideal place for recess and play time. It was also great fun to swing through the racks for lumber. We were especially excited to find a tunnel under the school office where the scales had the weights and measures for loads that would pull up to the lumberyard window. There was a tube through which some of the scale equipment worked and a large hose attached to it. The students discovered they could put the hose to their ear and hear everything that was said by the teacher, Miss Austin, in the office.

The favorite time for Miss Austin to discipline the students with her paddle was at noon. She would say, "When you are ready for your discipline, tell me." If we waited until 1 p.m., the other students would witness paddlings. Jack Parrot dominated the listening tube until one day he was to be disciplined. That day he went to the sink in the office, filled a dipper with water, poured it down the tube, and Lindsay Atteberry got an ear full.

All the boys in our family were in the band and one day we arrived at the school early for practice. The school was locked, but Charles would not be denied entrance. He knew a window, he thought, that was always open. He scaled the wall of the school, to the French window in the library that was to be open. It was locked! He had no choice but to break the small, corner pane in the window and unlock it, crawl in and let his brothers in the building. There were many questions among staff and librarians about the broken window but until this book goes to press, no one will know how it was broken. For years we would drive past that old school building, see that little window still broken and live anew the daring and bravery of our oldest brother and our ability to keep secrets. These were some of the good days in Wilder school.

Foreclosures came to many farmers. Daddy had a farm in Sunny Slope, near Caldwell, offered him by the New York Life Insurance Company in Sunny Slope. This farm was in good repair with fences and out buildings; however, the house was quite small. We made large porches serve as bedrooms and a dining room. It afforded us the opportunity to live as neighbors to the Skeltons who were members of the church. Another neighbor was Mr. Marks. All the neighbors shared in putting up hay and threshing. This gave work for all the boys, and the big sheepmen in the state would contract fields to provide hay for their flocks. Daddy contracted to a man by the name of Mr. Andy Little.

Albert Hall was a new convert at church. Daddy and Mother made a home for him immediately, and he and my brother Charles hauled hay for Mr. Little. They carried guns because they could collect a bounty of $5.00 for the head of any dog found pulling wool on the sheep. Early one morning, Daddy called all the boys together and told us he had to take mother to the hospital in Nampa. She was pregnant, and the baby was about to be born. He gave us instructions for the day's work. Albert and Charles were to haul hay, while Bob and I were to tend to the milking and feeding. It was daylight as I approached the cow lot, and the chickens were picking grain from the manure. But, there was some new excitement. I spotted a dog shaking a chicken. I ran to the house, got father's gun and shot the dog. It did not die but headed up the road. I settled for a near miss and went about the chore of milking. In a couple of hours Charles went by Mr. Marks' farm. Marks greeted him and asked to see his gun. He told Charles someone had shot his dog with a twenty-two special. He let Charles go because he was carrying a twenty-two, but not a special. Marks did the same with Albert, and he also cleared the inspection.

Charles and Albert circled the barn and related Marks' charge to Bob and me. But, after we learned it was

Marks' dog, I swore Bob to secrecy about giving his dog "lead poison." About that time, Daddy returned from the Nampa Hospital to announce that we had a new baby sister, Ruth Esther. The joy of a new sister soon melted when Mr. Marks visited that evening. He had decided the dog was shot with a twenty-two and either Charles or Albert had done it. Furthermore, he declared that until they confessed their crime, he couldn't cooperate in haying or threshing time. Bob and I were never questioned about the incident, and it remained a well-kept secret between us from 1933 until a family reunion in 1948.

While we were on that farm, we had the luxury of having Bro. J.H. Altizer as our mail carrier. He sold Daddy his Texas buckskin horse and bought a Star touring car with the proceeds. There was no refrigeration in those days, hence, mother would phone Bro. Altizer (many of the neighbors did the same thing), and he would bring fresh meat and other staples to the ranch. The boys would give the Star car a first class inspection while mother paid the mailman and gave him bundles of goodies from her garden. The chrome radiator with the blue porcelain star on it was the item that took our attention.

On the days the men worked in the fields, I was assigned to bring water to the field for Daddy and the hired hands. Neighbors would have me bring them water too. (Daddy never allowed us to take money for errands.) One day the temptation was too great. Mr. Trunnel gave me a nickel, and I put it in my pocket. It burned my pocket and also my heart with guilt. A favorite place for the boys to sit in the evening was back of the wood box in the kitchen. That evening I was there alone, and I spotted a good place for the nickel — back of a one-by-twelve mop board. It was my plan just to stick it in the crack until morning then take it to school and buy a candy bar. I carefully and quietly slipped it in the crack and away it went to the bottom of that mop board. That investment in misbehavior remained back of that board, even after we moved to another farm.

We continued to get jobs working for neighbors. Mr. Vance wanted me to help drive the derrick team for one day. (Farmers paid a dollar a day.) When the day was finished, Mr. Vance tormented me by saying, "I do not pay my help until I have milked my cows." I knew it was Saturday night and my folks were waiting for me at the corner of Vance's farm. It seemed an eternity for him to finish milking. He finally finished and handed me a silver dollar. I ran through the clover field and jumped in the back seat of the old touring car. Dad said, "How much did he pay you?" I gladly told him, "One silver dollar." He wanted to see it. I felt in all my pockets and couldn't find it. Daddy related how he told mother that if I was paid in silver it would jump out of my pocket as I ran through the hay field. A few years later I saw Mr. Vance and told him I lost my first dollar in that field, and he said, "I am going home and plow that field today!"

Shortly thereafter, electricity came to the farms, and ours was no exception. We had electric lights, an electric motor on the Maytag washing machine, yard lights and an electric motor on the well pump. We had purchased a new cream separator, and it came in a wooden box which made a perfect cover for the well motor. We put an electric switch on the box, and it was great just to hit the switch with a bucket and watch the water flow. One day a great rain came. I hit the bucket against the switch and found myself abruptly knocked down and in the mud. My total lack of knowledge of electric power was manifest as I picked the bucket up with a stick and hung it on the pump, thinking the electricity was still in the bucket.

That farm had an irrigation ditch which circled the front yard, where the men and boys would rest after a noon meal. One hot summer day, a beautiful new car stopped by the yard. A tall, western-dressed man with cowboy boots, hat and suit got out of the car and asked for directions to a

16

neighbor's house. After he returned to his car, all the boys jumped the ditch to see where he was from. There it was as big as day and bright as the noonday sun, a license plate that read **T E X A S!!!** We had read about them, but this was our first time to see a real Texan. His dress, his car and his accent made a lasting impression on me. That day I told my brothers that some day I would go to Texas and see more men like him.

Times worsened, another corporation bought the farm, and the Guild family moved again. This time we settled southwest of Caldwell in the Dixie District, close to the Boise River. To earn a living, some of us worked in warehouses, while others farmed. The money we earned was pooled to keep the family together. Charles had trapped some, and, instead of working in the potato warehouses, he trapped the river and worked on the Tramune dairy farm. Neaoma and I worked in the warehouses, while Bob, Mary Ellen and Grace picked fruit and did other neighborhood jobs.

Fuel was expensive, so we cut wood to burn. Charles would gather sagebrush stumps. I walked the railroad tracks home from school and carried a sack so I could pick up pieces of coal. I became a common sight to the engineers and firemen. They learned what I was doing and would throw off a shovel or two of coal, and it would make this coal-picker's day. If I found a railroad tie that had been pulled, I would run home, saddle a horse and drag it to the house before some of the neighbors got it.

When I graduated from high school, I enrolled in the College of Idaho. After my first year in college, Charles and I answered the call from the Forest Service to fight fire on the Salmon River in Central Idaho. We could make as much as $12.00 a day as compared to $1.00 a day in the harvest. The experience was rewarding. The Forest Service had conscripted fifty hobos to the fire zone, and we worked with them. They soon learned that I was planning to attend a

17

Christian college and wanted to enter the ministry. They called me their "Sky Pilot." They believed I would keep fires away from our camp grounds and in turn they would carry the five-gallon water bag for me. Most of the fires were started with lightning. The hobos were good men, some with college degrees, but they were not religious. When the storms were splitting trees around us, some of them would stand up and shake their firsts at the storm and say, "Come and get us, we were here first!" or "Hit'er again Mr. Lightning."

Our food, clothes and shoes were brought to the camp by mule-train. We were allowed to order the foods we liked except ice cream. Prairie chickens were plentiful. We could rock them easily. The cook promised to clean and cook them on halves. We brought in a lot of them, and they went good in our noon lunch sacks. We were paid portal-to-portal pay, which meant we were able to save money. We worked hard. Some fires would take forty-eight or sixty hours to control. After they were controlled, we would walk the fire trails and put out smoldering embers. It was a valuable experience.

Later, during the war, 1943, five of the children were grown, and Daddy moved his family to a small farm he bought in the Tallman community near Albany, Oregon. He farmed it and worked at Veal and Sons Furniture Co., as well as the bureau of mines. For seven years he bought and improved homes in Albany and retired on a small acreage at Tanget, Oregon. He loved his children and made great sacrifices for them to attend public schools and college. He died March 24, 1950, and was buried in the Willamette Memorial Cemetery. Mother was buried by his side at the age of eighty-three on November 24, 1974. My father was a mature man before he obeyed the gospel and never took an outstanding public role in the church. He was, nevertheless, a vital force in a quiet way. On one occasion, the Caldwell men planned to cancel a meeting at the church for lack of funds. Daddy shared the shortage with the family and suggested he would take a sow pig and her litter to the Saturday sale. He received $55.00 after the commission was paid, took the amount the next Sunday and told the men to go ahead and plan for the spring meeting. He would send a half-beef to the neighbors many times. Once I questioned his generosity in the midst of the depression and he replied, "If it never comes back to me, it will come back to you kids." I have recalled many, many grocery showers, poundings and kitchen showers given to Sammie and me in our ministry, and I always thought of the outpourings of love as consistent with the generous spirit of my father, and it was coming back to his children.

Chapter 2

THE CONSEQUENCES
OF CLAUDE'S CONVERSION

It was puzzling to the whole family, especially to me, when J. C. Bailey told us there was not a single congregation of the churches of Christ in Montana and not a minister. It added to our concern when we moved to Idaho and found only four little churches in the entire state. However, we were fortunate to move near Caldwell where one of the churches was located. They had about thirty members, but no minister. (M. Loyd Smith, Lewiston, Idaho, was the only minister in the state.) When we inquired further, we discovered things were not better in Oregon and Washington. Oregon had six congregations with two ministers, Shelby Smith and Glenn Handy, and neither was full time. Washington had six congregations with J.C. Bunn paid by all the churches to travel among them to strengthen them and establish new congregations.

Our family subscribed to the Firm Foundation, published in Austin, Texas. From its pages we learned about hundreds of churches in Texas, Oklahoma, Arkansas and Tennessee. We longed to see larger fellowships and hear more of the Word preached.

At that time there was growing in my heart an idea that seemed impossible — could the Lord use a boy off the farm and the hills of Montana and Idaho as a preacher of the gospel? We read the Bible daily as a family and excitement came to my heart when we saw in the gospels that John the Baptist was a common man from the wilderness, and he preached. Jesus was a carpenter's son, and he became a preacher. I really became interested when we learned that Peter, Andrew, James and John came to the ministry from the fishing business.

There is no memory more vivid or more meaningful, more renewed in my lifetime and heart than that day we went to the Boise River and at the hands of J.C. Bailey I was baptized into Christ. A host of family and church friends witnessed it from the river bank. Afterwards, we returned home in the old Buick touring car. When the family went into the house, I lingered by the rear wheel of that old car and offered my first prayer. In simple terms I called on the Lord and said, "Lord, if you can use a boy from the farm to preach, I want to be a preacher. I want to help take the gospel to the Northwest and anywhere you want me to go. Please, Lord, show me the way to accomplish these desires. In Jesus name, Amen." My acceptance of Christ by faith, my turning from a world of sin and finding cleansing in the blood of Jesus through baptism and, finally, my new resolution, gave me great strength. I became more excited every time I went to church, and my heart continued to burn with desire to preach.

School was important to the parents of this large family. Mother had gone to Norwegian school seven years, and Daddy got to go to school four years until the violent deaths of his father and older brother when he had to help his mother run the farm and provide for the family. Therefore, both of them were determined to see their children go to school. Dad was interested in sports and wanted his boys to excel in them. Robert and I took up baseball, and Charles went on to play football. But we needed equipment, and it was very expensive in the depression years. A neighbor, Mr. Karnes, had a row-crop farm and put out onion sets in the spring. He offered seventy-five cents a row for setting out onions, and the rows were more than an eighth of a mile long. The four oldest children worked before and after school. I remember making ten dollars. That was a lot of money! I made a decision to buy a new ball glove for five dollars and a new American Standard Reference Bible with the other five.

High school and summers saw most of my time taken up with the baseball glove. I started at first base and later became a left-handed pitcher. Glenn Lundy, a member of the church, managed a semi-pro team, the Indiana Pirates, and invited me to play. This carried me into the College of Idaho, but baseball was short lived in college. My father learned that I had a few beers with the boys after games. Being a strong disciplinarian, he had a long talk with me, took my glove and told me I was through with baseball. "But I can't tell the coach, Dad!" "No," Dad said, "I'll go to college with you and tell him myself." Daddy did exactly that. He and I went back to the car. Daddy's heart was broken, and he wept openly and said, "Son, I had to do it and some day you will understand it."

A new door opened immediately. The Presbyterians had a department of Bible in the College of Idaho, and I enrolled under Professor James Millar. Many good things happened with this professor. James Millar gave me a job typing his Ph.D. dissertation, and I worked long hours. Mr. Millar looked pale and thin, and my mother always gave him vegetables and milk when he brought me home after work.

While I was attending the College of Idaho, the Caldwell church began calling on me to make talks. God was ruling all this time in my young life. Daddy had cut off the baseball, the five dollar Bible was getting attention, and Dr. Millar's papers, as well as his classes, were very informative. About that time a new person came to the Caldwell church. She was Sister Eppie Beasley Jones, a retired postmistress from Waldo, Arkansas. She had always wanted to be a missionary and after retirement she had corresponded with a Brother A.G. Sims in Caldwell and was encouraged to move to the Northwest. We needed this great lady. She taught in a quiet way. She showed the boys how to use their knives without carving their initials on the backs of pews and not to chew gum in church. She helped the men by getting them to wear a tie and coat. Her help to the ladies was never ending and valuable. She helped with their sewing, taught classes and had a very, very sweet spirit.

After one of my talks at church, Sister Jones took me aside and under her arm and said, "You do not belong in the College of Idaho; you belong in a Christian College." Well, all I had known or heard about Christian colleges was in the American Christian Review, edited by Daniel Somner, and he was opposed to Christian colleges. (Supporters of Daniel Somner's views were referred to as Somnerites.) One day I got catalogues in the mail from Abilene Christian College, David Lipscomb College and Harding College. Since Abilene was the closest to Idaho, I read with excitement how the board of trustees, staff and faculty were all members of the church. They had four hundred students and ninety-five percent of them were Christians. The day arrived to share my heart's desire with someone. I talked with my mother about what I wanted to do. I wanted to preach. This was thrilling to Mother. She told Daddy and we began making plans. As mentioned earlier, instead of working on the farms at a dollar a day the following summer, Charles and I took a job on the Salmon River fighting fire. We were paid fifty cents an hour, and it was portal-to-portal pay. I saved for bus fare to Abilene, clothes and had forty dollars to enter Abilene Christian College.

Leaving home for college was more than leaving the family. It involved going twenty-five hundred miles with little expectation of support from home and no federal loan programs. It meant leaving our first church family in distress over their favorite son going to a Christian college. There were no expectations about coming home Christmas. There were no funds. Because of the Somnerite influence, when I did return home the first two summers, the elders would not call on me to preach, pray or have any part. It was a different story during my senior year. V.E. Dart was in the eldership and took a kindly look at me. In fact, he walked across a hay field where I was mowing and handed me eighty dollars toward my schooling the next fall.

The turning point came when Weldon B. Bennett, a fellow student, came with me to Idaho and worked with the church in Pocatello. He became discouraged there, and I invited him up for a week at Caldwell. Boys in Idaho were like Texas boys; they liked to go to town on Saturday nights. There were no funds to go to a show or other places of entertainment. I always enjoyed the street corner singing of Mr. Urshan, a Pentecostal preacher, and his wife. Large crowds would gather. The night Weldon and I went to town, Mr. Urshan preached on two baptisms, water and Holy Spirit. He affirmed they were two-in-one and both for us today. Many Civil Conservation Corps boys would often attend and testify, and that night was no exception. Weldon said, "Hold my hat, I am going up there." He made his way through the crowd, asked to testify and Urshan gave him the stand. In the meantime, I spotted Brother J.H. Altizer, one of our elders, and I worked my way up to his side and said, "That young man is a friend of mine, Weldon B. Bennett, a classmate from Abilene Christian College." Weldon explained the Bible's position on baptism and among other things said, "I am from Texas and I have heard of two-in-one shoe polish and two-in-one oil, but I have never read about two-in-one baptism in the Bible. To the contrary I have read about just one baptism for us today and it is in the Bible, but I didn't bring my Bible." The audience yelled, "Let him use yours." Urshan handed Weldon his Bible, and he read from Ephesians 4:4-5, "There is one Lord, one faith, one baptism." The audience cheered, and Brother Altizer commended him that night and asked him to preach Sunday morning at the church. Altizer asked me to preach that night.

25

After the evening service, Altizezr said, "I have heard Gatewood from Salt Lake City, and I have listened to the two of you. I have been taught to believe that boys from our colleges were from a "preacher factory," and we should not use them because they do not preach the gospel. I have changed my mind."

God's will was working. Before many months passed the elders wrote me to plan to hold their summer meeting after graduation. When I returned home, I had a new bride, Sammie LaRue Lacy Guild. Sister Eppie Beasley Jones met us on the church porch and said, "I made the first investment in your degree and your wife. I mailed a penny post card to David Lipscomb College, Harding and Abilene Christian." Oh, how God was using that great woman to direct the lives of people including a young preacher for the Northwest.

There was much more to learn in college than lectures from volumes of books and well-informed professors. There were hundreds of young men interested in the same thing — to be trained to preach the word of God. Many of these students have become lifetime friends and pillars of support to the church and an encouragement to me: Weldon B. Bennett, Raymond C. Kelcy, Otis Gatewood, Batsell B. Baxter, Trine Starnes, Leroy Brownlow, M. Norvel Young, Le Moine Lewis, Jesse Young, Woodrow W. Hughes, Logan Buchanan, Fred Barton, Forrest Orr, John Stevens, Luther Savage, L.D. Webb, Arnold Watson, Bernard Passmore, Joe Laird, Frank Traylor and others. Many of the faculty and administration were helpful in the ministries of Sammie and me: W.R. Smith, Don H. Morris, James F. Cox, Walter H. Adams, Charles H. Roberson, Robert Bell, Lawrence Smith and others. They followed our ministries into British Columbia, Alaska, the Northwest, India, Africa, Germany and two Christian colleges: Ft. Worth Christian College and Columbia Christian College.

The daily chapel services were important to the first Idaho student to attend Abilene Christian. Our family had met once a week in our home in Montana, and when we moved to Idaho it was shocking to hear Brother Altizer announce services on both Sunday and Wednesday nights. At Abilene Christian College we met every day for a worship service. Although it was a new experience, daily chapel quickly became a "soul-food" experience. I also found it shocking when Brother Bradshaw, manager of the batching house where I lived with twenty-two preacher boys, asked if I would like to go to church with him or somewhere else. I replied, "Oh, I go to the church of Christ." Bradshaw said, "I do too but there are seven congregations of the church of Christ in Abilene." This was very strange because there were only four congregations in the whole state of Idaho, and one West Texas town had seven in it.

I chose to go to the College church with Brother Bradshaw. He introduced me to his barber, the banker, the president of the college and other local businessmen. It did not seem quite right to me because all the members at Caldwell were farmers except Brother Altizer, the mail carrier. Services were beyond me that first Sunday morning. Brother McKenzie lead the singing and the parts: base, tenor, soprano and alto came to my ears like tides from the sea. It was beautiful. I had never heard anything like it. The preaching by Brother O.A. Colley was great. Communion was also a new and surprising experience. They used trays with individual glasses in them. I had only used or had seen a pitcher of grape juice poured into two glasses and members drinking from the same cup. Individual glasses were completely unexpected. The friendliness of the members and a congregation of eight hundred people, compared to the thirty back home, was a bit overwhelming but a joyous and delightful experience. Immediately after the morning services, I went to my room, wrote home and said, "I have found heaven outdoors."

27

Bradshaw's boarding house was just right for college boys. Lewis Stivers of Los Angeles, California, and I were the last to arrive at the house. There were no more rooms left, but Bro. Bradshaw graciously backed his model A Ford out of the single garage, put a window and door in the front, installed a gas burner, and put in a couple of tables and a bed on the dirt floor. It became our home for a semester. With twenty-two boys living in a house there were all kinds of backgrounds and personalities represented and just as many stories to be told. Jesse Young stayed at Bradshaw"s. He was older but serious about his school work. He took up with me, and we agreed to study Greek five hours a day. This was an experience of great worth.

An experience of much less lasting value involved another roomer, Ariel Shepherd, from the hill country of Texas. He tried to be one hundred percent Texas and country. He had an encounter or two with the boys that roomed three blocks south of us at the Crockett house. In a few days the Crockett boys dumped a sack of cats at Bradshaw's. When we cooked, the cats would climb the screen doors and beg for food. They tried Shepherd's screen door. In his big and brave Texas disposition, he pulled each cat off the screen by the tail and hit it with the hammer. That was the end of the cat crop.

Bro. Bradshaw was a cabinet maker, and W.A. Pheifer enjoyed using his tools. One day W.A. tried his hand on the lathe. It jerked the board through, his hand dropped on the blades and four or five slices of each finger were in the shavings. Brother Bradshaw rushed him to the hospital and several boys got the nice round slices of his fingers and mounted them on a plaque and hung it over his bed as a trophy.

During this time, the depression was very real, and each administrator and faculty member had a cow staked in his back yard. (There were not many houses on the ACC hill at that time.) President Cox had a cow. One evening she

28

had pulled her stake and was coming down the road in front of Bradshaw's. Shepherd took hold of her rope, led her down the driveway and announced, "It is time to milk." All the boys came with pans, bottles and cups and drained the old Jersey's crankcase. Bradshaw was sitting on his porch and got a good laugh out of the whole affair.

Each boy at the Bradshaw house did his own laundry. There were no washing machines or dryers, but there was a wash board and tub. It was a challenge to put out the best looking wash. After pinning it on the line, we would go to the library to study. Fellow bachelors would watch for the owner of the wash. When they saw him coming they would soak his clothes with the hose. It was all taken in good fun.

The second semester I had Woodrow W. Hughes of Tuttle, Oklahoma, as a roommate. All our funds were gone, so Woodrow and I wrote our parents but with little avail. The potato crop had failed in Idaho, and my parents could not send any money. Woodrow heard from his parents in the form of a sack of cracked wheat. We soaked it at night and cooked it three times a day. Finally, we decided to go to Dean Adams' office and stay there until we got a job. The Dean did a lot of phoning but with no success. Finally the Dean said, "I have a cow and I can milk her. But, to help that cracked wheat, I'll give each of you a quart of milk if one of you will milk her in the morning and the other at night. I did the morning milking, and Woodrow did the evening job. It was a treat to have milk with the cracked wheat! However, one morning I went to milk, and to my horror the grainery door had been left open. In the night, the cow had eaten the grain, foundered and lay dead in the lot. It had fallen to me to tell the Dean that we had killed his cow. Dean Adams came to look, and I remember to this very day what the Dean said, "And she was a registered Jersey."

By this time the Dean found us a job on Jenkins' Dairy near McMurray College. There was no money to pay us, but they gave us board, room, laundry and transportation. We

29

would milk twenty-five cows night and morning. We jumped at the job just to get enough to eat. This job went great until Woodrow fell ill. Dr. John Paul Gipson, the college physician, was called. He examined Woodrow and announced he had appendicitis and would have to go to the hospital for surgery. An ambulance was called. This was another new experience for us. I was invited to ride in the ambulance with Woodrow and on the way Woodrow said, "Claude, make out a list of the songs I want sung at my funeral." Well, he got well and finished the school year and at this writing he is in good health.

Preacher boys talked all the time about getting a church and starting to preach. L.D. Webb and I didn't have a church the first year, nor did we know much about preaching. Therefore we preached at the county jail. It was a good experience. When Christmas came, I could not go home, but L.D. was invited to hold a meeting for his home church in Post Oak, Oklahoma. He didn't have enough sermons for a meeting, hence he invited me to go along. The church agreed that one of us would preach every other night. We stayed at L.D.'s home. His mother had died and his daddy was blind. Food was very, very common in their home and between meals we would shell peanuts out of the peanut hay in the barn. It was there and then L.D. declared, "I hope the Lord will help me get so far away from this place that they cannot reach me with a three-cent stamp." The meeting closed with two baptisms and a few restorations.

The church had promised to provide our train fare only. After we bought the tickets each of us had a dime. We bought two oranges and rode most of the day on the oranges, but it didn't matter. We had baptized two people, and we felt as big as G.C. Brewer and Foy E. Wallace, Jr. When we arrived at our rooms at the college there was a Christmas box from my parents. A feast was spread. We had fruit cake, cookies, nuts and a jar of jam. We ate the whole shipment that night. Offering thanks that evening was special. We had held a meeting, baptized people, traveled home safely and enjoyed a good meal at the end of the road.

God's hand was directing me to know great churches in Texas and wonderful Christians. At the beginning of my second year in Abilene, Bro. Grimsley, an elder of the college church, talked to me about going to a little town forty miles away, Cross Plains, Texas. Scores of preacher boys thumbed their way to preaching appointments. I thumbed my way to Cross Plains. M.C. Baum and M.A. White were elders and great men in the community. They liked what they heard, and I fell in love with them. Consequently, we entered into an agreement. I would come every other Sunday, and they would give me the contribution the Sundays I came.

It was a joy to be associated with people who were patient with me, and I had the opportunity to preach the things I was learning at the college. The home-cooked meals were great and lots of boys would go with me just to have a good Sunday dinner. The elderly people were well read in the scriptures and when I made mistakes they would correct me. One time I told about the death angel passing over the children of Israel. A wonderful grandmother took me aside and pointed out that it was God who passed over them, not a death angel.

Pioneer, Texas, was ten miles east of Cross Plains. The Pioneer church arranged their services so I could come and preach for them in the afternoons on the Sundays I went to Cross Plains. The contributions were about ten to twelve dollars a week in Cross Plains and two to five dollars at Pioneer.

The school year ended without a single baptism at Cross Plains. I offered my resignation, thinking someone else could do a better job. Bro. Baum said, "Let's wait and see about this. You come early this fall and hold our August meeting." That meeting brought the fruit. There were twenty-seven baptisms and fifteen restorations. Some of

31

the baptisms were Curtis Strickland, grocery clerk; Melvin Plockie, postmaster (he later became a very fine minister); V.A. Underwood, vocational agriculture teacher; and little Billy Henderson. The offerings soon jumped to about twenty-five dollars a week.

The members took me into their homes and showed me many kindnesses. One Sunday I had dinner with Sister Waggoner. She saw that my shirt had the elbows worn out, so after dinner she said, "Claude you go in that bedroom, take that shirt off, take a nap and I'll fix your sleeves." She put nice patches on the shirt sleeves and turned the collar. It was just like a new shirt. Others would stick a jar of jelly in my pocket, give me a sack of peanuts or watermelons. This group not only heard me preach but adopted me. By this time I had a twenty-eight model Chevy. Bro. White would have me bring a number of boys to help with the singing, and we stayed at his place. Sister White was a good cook. She would fix sliced tomatos and black-eyed peas and run some chickens out from under the wood pile to fry. To finish it off in style, they would get out the hand-crank freezer and make ice cream. Brother White had a great variety of song books, and we would sing till 10 o'clock. Finally, he would say, "Cut it off boys, we have to get our rest for Sunday and Mother must put down the 'baptist pallets.'" These mats were laid like cord wood on the floor for our beds, and we would have another great week at Cross Plains, Texas.

I mentioned earlier a 1928 Chevrolet. It was time for my brother, Robert, and a friend from the Caldwell church, Arnold Watson, to enter Abilene Christian College. My father thought it best we buy a used car and save bus fare. Mr. Stubblefield had a used car lot and agreed to sell me the 1928 Chevrolet for seventy dollars. He didn't want a contract when he learned I was studying for the ministry. He told me to just mail him a five or ten dollar bill whenever I could. It needed a paint job, and we did a good job with a brush. We painted the body green and the wheels yellow. The top needed repair, but the engine was good. It would do forty miles an hour and was very good on gasoline. It took us a week to drive to Abilene, and once there it provided transportation for my preaching appointments.

Clyde, Texas, fifteen miles from Abilene, heard about my preaching in Cross Plains. Arrangements were made for me to come two Sundays a month, and they also agreed to give me the collection on those Lord's days. (One of the members was a sixth grader, Billy Sol Estes.) Earl Hayes was an elder and ran a dairy. He was also on the Board of Trustees at Abilene Christian College. He had several boys, and Conard was in my class. We spent many weekends in Clyde riding calves in the Hayes' pasture, milking cows and enjoying the Pyeatt, Cotton, Waggoner families and many others, including Norma and Forrest Orr. All these families became a great part of our lives.

A number of our religious papers carried the report of the Cross Plains meeting. From that date forward I had more calls for revival meetings than I could fill. I also preached each Sunday for the duration of my college career. My senior year in college I served five churches: Cross Plains, Pioneer, Clyde and on fifth Sundays I would preach morning and night at Acuff and afternoons at Owens, Texas.

It is easy to recall my first appointment at Acuff and Owens. Weldon B. Bennett's folks had a store in Lubbock, and I was to stay with them. Because of the depression, they were unable to afford a telephone, and I could not call them to make arrangements for my first night's stay. Therefore, I had to make some arrangements for a hotel, and I had no money. I found a flop-house that rented cots for twenty-five cents a night. I was happy that I had a quarter, and I took my cot with a burlap curtain separating me from other men, most of whom were hobos. I had worked with men such as these in the forest service fighting fire, and I was not afraid of them. However, in the night there was a commotion that wakened everyone. The manager informed us to put on our shoes if we didn't want them stolen. (One man had already lost his shoes.) I finished the night, hitchhiked to Acuff and preached without breakfast. Fortunately, I was able to drive my own car on subsequent trips. A Mr. Davis owned a store and service station at Acuff, and he would always fill my tank. This was a great help. On one of my trips, I had a flat tire and my spare was ruined. I found a Dunlop Tire Store and told them my story. The manager listened patiently and inquired, "Do you know Don H. Morris at Abilene Christian College? He was my speech teacher at Abilene High School. How many tires do you want?" Since he trusted me because of Don H. Morris, who later became President of Abilene Christian College, I have been a life-long friend of Dunlop tires.

Abilene Christian had a great influence on my life. Teachers taught for little support; their dress, rough hands and down-to-earth mannerisms made me believe they were honest, hard-working people, and they were. Bro. Robert C. Bell impressed me with his big hands and gentle nature. The white hair of Charles H. Roberson, his scholarship and his requirements in memory work made us respect him.

Brother Roberson was in his seventies, and he looked well and strong. He had patented jokes he told in all his classes, and the students had a thing going; the way to get a grade was laugh at all his jokes. Here is a sample: "Do you know why I stay healthy?" We would reply, "Tell us all about it." He would say, "When Mrs. Roberson and I married we entered into an agreement that if we quarreled I would take a walk. It seems through these years the outdoors has agreed with me." He would immediately ask if we knew how Mrs. Roberson stayed so slim and trim? His reply, "She stays that way by jumping at conclusions and stacking up bills."

Mrs. Clarence Bailey, an English professor, was a great teacher and sympathetic toward boys and girls who were a long way from home. Twice in my first year in Abilene, she and her husband invited me to their place to eat. It was a great time of fellowship and a great treat. Mrs. E.D. Walker, a science professor, was excellent in her field and a great disciplinarian. My minor was in biological science and genetics. In one of her courses several of us were having difficulty. G.C. Brewer, minister at the Broadway church of Christ in Lubbock, was asked to hold the spring meeting. (The college always had two gospel meetings per year.) They believed in those days that evangelism was important even among non-member students. Brother Brewer was advertised as the preacher in the brotherhood best informed on the sciences. One of his sermons was "Science and the Bible." All the genetic students were amazed as he recited scientific data as though he had memorized our textbook. His sermons challenged us to study longer and harder.

Preacher students were required to take courses in platform art and church music. These classes took the "hayseed" and "country" ways and habits from most of the boys. They acted and looked like true tradesmen in the pulpit. Such classes would be good for ministerial students today. In those days, many churches did not have song leaders. Therefore, the preacher was expected to lead the singing. They taught us how to get the pitch and to direct four-four, six-eight and three-four time. These two courses have been valuable to me these fifty-four years.

The college had a practice of having the senior class select two preacher boys to preach what they called the "Senior sermons." The class of 1939 selected Irvin Driskill and me. This was a total surprise to me, because I had only been in Abilene three years and as far as I knew I was the only preacher in the history of my family. It meant that Irvin and I would not have to answer the five hundred Bible questions required of Bible majors. Bro. Roberson, Chairman of the Department of Bible, would assign the subject and when it was delivered at the College church of Christ, a speech, English and Bible teacher would grade us. My subject was "The Certainties of Jesus." I developed four major points: Jesus was certain of God , His mission, His Kingdom and the needs of humanity. After the sermon, I was awarded an "A," and it was the best night of my life in the ministry. Being a country boy and coming so far from the Bible-belt, it was was also exciting to be elected by the faculty to the "Who's Who in American Universities and Colleges."

Dean Walter H. Adams, just before graduation, called me to his office and offered me two pulpit jobs. They were in Coleman and Quannah, Texas. Both places had good buildings and a parsonage and sizeable memberships. I remembered my commitment to the Northwest and had corresponded with the church in Yakima, Washington. They had never had a preacher and when I inquired as to the extent of their membership, George Halley wrote, " To be specific, we have twenty-one members; fourteen alive and seven dead." I chose to go to Yakima.

The greatest single blessing that came to me at Abilene Christian College, was to meet and marry Sammie LaRue Lacy from Warren, Oklahoma. A student representing Southwestern Company in Nashville, Tennessee, was selling Bibles in her community and when he learned that she was ready for college, he sold her on Abilene Christian College.

I am sure God's providence had a part in our meeting and marrying. Just prior to my senior year, the college administration asked me to come to school early, along with others, to help enroll the freshman class. There was a great lineup of students. The very first day I helped Sammie LaRue enroll. That evening I hurried to my room and declared to my brother, Bob, and Arnold Watson, "I have

36

been blessed to meet a most wonderful girl from Oklahoma. She is beautiful, her background is like mine, she comes from a farming family, she loves the church and she has everything going for her." I had found a new interest, and it was to make her a part of my life and my dream to carry the gospel into all the world.

Sammie had told her friends she wanted to get off the farm and get enough education to do something that would at least take her to Altus, Oklahoma, fifteen miles from her home. She was invited into ACC's drill team, the "Kitten Club." She was very neat in her uniform as she paraded on the football field with the others. (As far as I was concerned, she looked as good in that group as though they were the Dallas Cowboys cheerleaders.) She wore pretty little frocks and patent leather shoes. She loved to come to Mission Study Class. (Preacher boys considered girls who attended as fair game for preacher's wives.) Sister Cogdell, her dorm supervisor, gave her senior privileges since she was dating a senior. In a matter of two months she was allowed to go with me to my preaching appointments. Arnold Watson was dating Ruby Mae White, an Abilene girl, and as we double dated, we spent a lot of time at her home.

Sammie's step-father was an elder in Warren, Oklahoma, and I was invited to preach for one of their fifth Sunday services. I got to meet the family, and they got to meet me. Later that fall, after a football game, I shared with Sammie my complete plans for evangelism, especially in the Northwest. It was time to let her know that I would love to have her in my future and dropped the question to this beautiful Oklahoma Christian girl, "Would you like to share with me in a life of evangelism?" Her answer was in the affirmative, and I replied, "We will keep our engagement confidential until we talk to your parents." Sammie has always said, "When he asked that question and I answered it, I thought 'What have I said?'" We made plans to visit her family again and ask their blessing in what we planned to do. There was a meeting of minds, even with her grandparents.

Her mother was neat and pretty. (I had been told to look at her mother and you will know what your wife will look like in later life.) There certainly has been no problem with this issue. Sammie and her mother are still very pretty women. Her step-father, B.T. Lacy, was a successful farmer, an elder in the church, and a man with a great sense of humor. I even liked her ten-year-old sister, Edna Lea. She later attended Abilene Christian College and married Albert Randall. They now live in Edna, Texas, where Albert farms and is an elder of the church.

The family had a strong church background. Grandmother Curry was a Billingsley and a first cousin to Price Billingsly, a pioneer preacher. I had never known a grandmother in my family, and it was a delight to know this great woman and her husband. They were Oklahoma farmers but had also been missionaries in Mexico. It was exciting to hear them recite stories of their work in a mission field.

The Curry history in the church, mission work with a number of families in Mexico, and their roots in Alabama were of great interest to me. I was also interested in hearing about Sammie's blood father, Samuel Lafaette Hammon. He was in World War One and contracted T.B. It was shortly after returning home from the war and his marriage to Velma O. Curry that he learned he had tuberculosis. In a relatively short time after their marriage, he had to go to New Mexico to a sanatorium. Sammie La Rue was born to them four months before his untimely death. Sammie's mother was widowed four years before meeting and marrying Beverly Tucker Lacy. He had three daughters of a former marriage, Bonnie, Lucille and Lila. His wife had died and a new union was formed to bring together four girls at their wedding.

Mother Curry was very well versed in the Bible and did a good job feeling me out if I was really grounded in all the vital principles of New Testament Christianity.

38

Sammie's Uncle Weldon had just married and was farming with his father. Later he farmed in Oregon, worked in Pueblo, Colorado, served the church as an elder, went to Bear Valley School of Preaching and has preached many years in Colorado and Oklahoma. Sammie's Aunt Esta was married to D. McCombs. They were always referred to as D and Esta. Sammie and her cousins picked up on the names of this favorite aunt and uncle, and they vowed that whoever had the first girl would name her D'Esta. This came true in our household with great delight. Later I got to meet her uncle Lee and aunt Stella. This aunt lived in Pueblo, and her home became a favorite stopping place between the northwest and Texas.

The blessing upon our engagement came from her family, and great plans were made for the wedding. By this time many calls were coming for my services in preaching work. Meetings would go thirty days in some places. I was booked to hold meetings in Caldwell, Idaho; Prosser, Sunnyside, Yakima and Goldendale, Washington; Cross Plains, Burkett and Cottonwood, Texas. There was also the added pressure of finals for my senior year at Abilene Christian College. Not knowing the heavy schedule of preaching, Sammie had thought about a June wedding. June was already assigned to Idaho and Washington. We set the date for March the twenty-second, 1939. Sammie took her spring break early and prepared for the wedding. Sister Glenn Green, the minister's wife in Altus, helped her with the plans. Sammie and her mother shopped for a dress. It was a beautiful blue dress (it is still in our possession) and all the other trappings for a wedding including pear blossoms from the trees in their pasture and orchard. It was held at the ranch house with all the kinfolks present. Money was difficult to come by, and, the Lord as my witness as I write, I had used all my money to rent an apartment at the Duckworth residence, buy a new suit and make the trip to Oklahoma. I paid Bro. Green the last five dollar bill I owned. (He gave it back to Sammie, and I believe he knew how poor we were from experience.) My credit card was good for gasoline to return to college and my preaching jobs. As soon as I returned to Cross Plains, Pioneer and Clyde to preach, they increased my pay for preaching because I had a new bride. Grocery showers were given in all three places. We had groceries under the bed and stacked in all the corners. We made an arrangement to trade extra sugar and lard for fresh meat and eggs at a little grocery, the Prune Shop, and life was going on with even better prospects than either of us expected.

Meanwhile, I had a job during my senior year sweeping and cleaning the offices of the President, James F. Cox; Vice President, Don H. Morris; and Bursar, Lawrence L. Smith. These were great men and great preachers. I learned things pushing a broom for them that later was helpful for me when I assumed leading administrative positions with two of our Christian colleges. Often they would hold conferences in a single office and the conversation would go like this: "I'll preach in San Angelo," Bro. Cox would say, "Lawrence, you will preach in Sweetwater. Bro. Don, you preach in Spur. We must impress the people that their checks this weekend are vital to keep from having the electricity cut off at the college." Such conversations were overheard often, and I know from this accidental information that colleges operated on very thin budgets. Let me add right here, one of the greatest teachers I ever had was Don H. Morris. He was my speech teacher and also my debating coach. I credit Bro. Morris with a major part of the training I received and for whatever good I have done on a common platform in preaching and also in debate.

Our fortunes changed rapidly and in multiple ways. Sammie's mother had been thoughtful and kept in a separate account the part of the pension funds Sammie received as a result of her father's death. Sister Lacy had only paid for Sammie's clothes and schooling from the fund. It was a

40

complete surprise to Sammie, and especially to me, that she had a check given her from the fund for five hundred fifty dollars. Mother Lacy advised us to buy a new car since we would be travelling in our meeting work. We traded my old 1928 Chevrolet for a new 1939 business coupe Chevrolet and only paid five hundred dollars difference. Imagine, a senior in college, a new wife, a new car and both of them paid for! Later, Mother Lacy revealed that she had loaned one thousand dollars to a man in Altus to buy a home. This money was returned to Sammie in 1941, and we were able to buy furnishings we had wanted and pay for our babies as they came along.

When graduation time arrived, Mother Lacy began her plans to attend the ceremonies. We were able to pay for our fees, cap and gown but had no cash to host this great lady from Oklahoma. I had worked two summers selling Bibles for Southwestern Company. I wired the home office in Nashville, Tennessee, and had them send me three hundred dollars worth of Bibles in care of Brother Bob Price, a recent convert who came to church in Pioneer but lived in Rising Star. (I chose this town because it was an oil town, and I thought they would have money.) I left my bride and drove to Rising Star. The Bibles were there, and the Price family let me live with them while I sold the Bibles. In three days I had sold all the Bibles and had one hundred twenty dollars in my pocket. It was enough to entertain Mother Lacy and make our trip to Idaho to start our meeting work.

It is a joy to recall names of men who graduated the same day and became great churchmen: Forrest Orr, Otis Garner, Weldon Bennett, Hugo Blackstone, Ferris Bryant, Cecil Huff, Elmo McCook, Hollis Smith, John Stevens, T.H. Tarbet, Paul McClung and others. That day could never have come to pass had it not been for the prayers and encouragement of many. I think of the days when my parents sold laying hens to send me funds, when V.E. Dart walked across the field, a Caldwell elder, and handed me

41

eighty dollars. Those dollars spoke to the college expenses, but they also said, "The elders at Caldwell now believe in what you plan to do."

This chapter of history cannot be complete without mentioning Arthur B. Tenney, the first preacher in Caldwell. By this time, God's providence directed a fine man to move to Caldwell to work as a proofreader at Caxton's Printers, the largest press in Idaho. He was a member of the church, reared at Graton, California, and attended the academy there. He had a Masters degree from Stanford University, was well schooled in the Bible, and they allowed him to preach simply because he didn't have a degree from a Christian college. He was on the firing line to help me see my way through Abilene. He would send funds personally and sometimes include funds he had solicited from individuals. His voice of assurance meant much to me and to our family that I was on the right track. It was Arthur B. Tenney that helped Caldwell get through the one-cup issue and begin using communion trays. He helped us see the value of good Bible School literature, encouraged Walter Skelton to preach, and took several of us to a Presbyterian music teacher to learn to lead singing.

I recall Tenney telling me about a visit by a fellow preacher from Texas whom he knew. This preacher asked Tenney how his work was going. He related that he had had forty or fifty baptisms in the year, but Tenney replied, "I haven't baptized a single soul, but I have had a great year." The Texas preacher was puzzled. It was then that Tenney told him, "When I came here two elders' wives were not speaking and had not spoken to each other in a long time. I now have them reconciled. They sit together and sing out of the same song book." The Texas preacher understood, and that was A.B. Tenney and his strength of reconciliation. He sent funds to me once in a while on the mission fields. He lived to teach at Abilene Christian College, preach in a number of churches and was in his nineties when he died.

42

He was a great man to encourage young preachers, to print and circulate tracts and in his optimism to see a church with a great future.

Chapter 3

NORTHWEST EVANGELISM

In my studies at Abilene Christian College, the ministerial students researched the history of restoration preachers in America. This search encouraged me because these men laid plans and had visions of fields unconquered with the gospel. Plans were laid, and they marched forward by faith to see the seed sown, converts made and churches established. This study assured me that dreaming and planning for a ministry in the great Northwest was not beyond my reach with the help of God. I want it to be part of the record today that I had dreams and visions and all of them came to pass, yea, even more than I really expected.

It was a high Sunday when the meeting started in Caldwell, Idaho, in June of 1939. My bride was introduced to all the home folks at church. (My parents, brothers and sisters had never met Sammie.) We stayed on the ranch with the folks. My sisters told me later about going into our room while we were in town and trying on Sammie's clothes and shoes. They enjoyed every minute of it, and they were enchanted by this newest member of the Guild family. It was love at first sight for all my family.

One highlight of the meeting were the baptisms. There were nine, and they included Bill Free and Orville Evans. They were baptized in the Boise River, and the water was cold. Little did I know then that God would use the three of us, Free, Evans and Guild to serve on the Board of Trustees at Columbia Christian College in Portland, Oregon. Bill Free's father followed A.B. Tenney at Caldwell as the minister. Today Bill Free and Orville Evans serve as elders at Caldwell. There have been many turns in the road for this great church through the years. One has been their attitude toward colleges. They now send monthly support to the Bible Department of Columbia Christian College.

Sammie and I moved on schedule to Prosser, Washington, for the next revival. Several were converted there, including Pauline Cowles. Throughout these fifty years of evangelism, Pauline has supported our efforts, and she and her husband, Jerry, are personal friends of ours. Pauline's baby daughter, Kay, is married to David Vanlandingham, minister for the church in San Diego, California. Myra Writer, a member at Prosser, also became a vital part of our lives. She was bedfast perhaps the last thirty years of her life but faithfully supported our mission efforts with contributions.

Our next meeting was in Sunnyside, Washington. The church met in a school house and didn't have electric lights. The Banton and Morrow families were leading in the work and continued to lead, even when they moved to Eugene, Oregon.

The time arrived for the meeting in Yakima. We brought all our earthly possessions in the Chevy business coupe and settled in Yakima, Washington, to become the first minister for the church there. They had raised a building shell at the Corner of Lennox and Cornell. The sub-flooring had knot holes in it, and the cold winds blowing up through the floor kept people awake. The church extended every courtesy possible to make us feel at home. Sister Bill Wilson lived on a ranch and seemed to sense our needs, especially when Sammie became pregnant. She furnished us with produce from their farm. (We got to see her husband, Bill, obey the gospel.) Our support was seventy-five dollars a month — ten dollars from the church in Altus, Oklahoma, and sixty-five dollars from Bro. George Pepperdine.

46

Converts came very fast. The first convert in Yakima was a young lady, Ruth Riddle. Mr. Rose and his daughter, both Catholics, obeyed the gospel. Homer Duggins and others of his family were baptized. Harley Riddle, a professional wrestler, was baptized. Mr. John Nance was another early convert. God was using our efforts for future plans for the Northwest. We helped with the wedding of Homer and Ann Loofborrow, and Homer later became a member of the Board of Trustees at Columbia Christian College.

People in Yakima were among many who had moved west because of the World War II clouds that were blowing. It brought growth to the church, but there were many barriers to cross. We had difficulty getting all the brethren to see that a baptistry was not a violation of scripture. We had to solve many problems such as individual communion cups, Bible school literature, and women teachers in Sunday school.

Yakima served as our base of operations as calls came to establish new congregations in other communities. During the Thanksgiving Lectureship at Caldwell, Idaho, we were approached to help start the work in Boise, Idaho. Sister McCoy from Lubbock, Texas, and Sister Bill Jenkins from Snyder, Texas, were the two ladies asking for help. We agreed to go the next spring, 1940, and help them.

The meeting began in the Jenkins' home. Invitations were sent out, Sammie and I did a lot of door knocking and in five days we had the house full. Mr. Jenkins had installed a furnace and stoker in the Lutheran building and inquired why we didn't rent their building. He asked me to go with him and on this special day the Lord was really leading. Mr. Jenkins did the talking and said, "This young man is doing some reorganizational work for the churches of Christ, and we would like to rent your building for two weeks." They agreed to the arrangement except on Sunday morning when they had their service. The charges were fifty dollars for fuel and the janitor's fee. (If I had been talking I would

47

have said, "We want to hold a gospel meeting," and they would not have opened their building.)

Where would we find the fifty dollars? The next morning I went to Mr. Jenkins and told him I didn't have the money. I explained that I had written the six churches in Idaho to help and only Midvale answered my letter, and they said they couldn't help. This great man said, "Don't worry about it. Here's a check; go pay the rent." Can you imagine the Lord using a nonmember to pay the rent when six churches failed to answer the call? The Lord works his wonders to behold!

The meeting went eighteen days. There were eighteen baptisms, including Mr. Jenkins and Mr. McCoy. Eighteen were restored from the Christian church, and the Lord had an answer for a preacher to hold them together. My mail was being forwarded from Yakima and in it was a letter from Charlie Johnson of Cheyenne, Wyoming. He stated, "I have full support from Texas, but in this congregation I am a square plug in a round hole. Do you know of a place that needs a Texas preacher?" We phoned him, and he was on the ground before we left.

It is interesting to know why Mr. McCoy could be reared in Lubbock, Texas, have folks attend and hold membership at the Broadway church and yet had not obeyed the gospel. I asked him about it and here is what happened. He worked at the ice plant, and there was always a great rush in his work after church services on Sunday mornings. (Everyone had an ice box at home. There were no electric refrigerators.) In the traffic on one Sunday morning, John T. White, minister at Broadway, came for his block of ice after church and said, "Son, I didn't see you in Sunday school today." He expressed his full feelings about that job and the church people getting ice when he replied, "Brother White, if there were not so many damned preachers in line to get ice on Sunday morning I could be in Sunday school." He was afraid to go back to church at Broadway after that encounter.

48

You might want to know my pay for that meeting in Boise. Since the six churches in Idaho didn't reply to my appeal for help, there was not a dime contributed to the efforts of the two of us in that great meeting. But, wait a minute. I got the best revenue check from the Lord I ever received in a meeting. Among those who were baptized was a family by the name of Hamm. They had a beautiful daughter, Phauneal, who was also baptized. When I returned to Yakima I had a letter from my brother, Robert Franklin, and the Air Force was transferring him to Boise. He was unmarried, and I told him to be sure and look up Phauneal Hamm. He found her, courted and married her. I got a fine sister-in-law, three nephews and two nieces out of that meeting, and that was worth far more than money.

While in a meeting that same summer in San Antonio, Texas, a new convert, Bro. Harry Graham, a wholesale fruit and vegetable dealer, approached me about helping with the work in the Northwest. He offered me funds for radio work wherever I traveled in mission meetings. I immediately signed a contract with a radio station in Yakima and got immediate results. Ladies in White Swan, Washington, had been listening to Otis Gatewood on KSL, Salt Lake City. They listened to our broadcast and found we were teaching the same thing. One lady was the superintendent of the Methodist Sunday school. She phoned and wanted us to study together. I agreed to come if she would set up a study with interested people. When we arrived, her home was filled to overflowing. We spent the whole day, and when evening came and the class was over we took two carloads of people to Yakima and immersed them for the remission of sins.

Ruth and Harley Riddle were mentioned earlier. Their mother, Sis. Effie Riddle, was a great mother to all of us, especially to Sammie when D'Esta was born. This great event took place July 6, 1940. Dr. Mullinnex, M.D., became involved in a debate I had in Yakima with the Seventh Day Adventists. (That was his church affiliation.) Since D'Esta was our first child, we debated whether we should continue with the same Adventist doctor. We decided to continue with his services, and to add injury to insult, D'Esta was delivered on the Sabbath day!

D'Esta was interested in books from the very beginning. Dolls were not her interest, nor were little friends, rocking chairs or her play pen. She always wanted us to read to her. She is still a great student and is well informed in the Bible. She has her M.A. degree in English and is Dean of Students at Pepperdine University. Her husband, Stuart Love, holds his Doctor's degree, is a great gospel preacher and teaches religion at Pepperdine. They have recently published a book, along with their older son, Mark, <u>Good News For Marriage</u>. It deserves a place in every home. (Order from: D.M.S. Communications, 24334 Baxter Dr., Malibu, Ca., 90265.) They have two sons. Mark ministers for a church in Arlington, Texas, and Jon is a medical doctor doing a residency in pediatrics in Little Rock, Arkansas. Stuart and D'Esta have two grandsons, our first great-grandsons, Zachary and Joshua.

We received word from Richland, Washington, that they wanted to start the church in the Tri-city area. Sammie and I answered the call, rented an old Lutheran building, and the church was established. Three great ladies played a part in that endeavor. They were Sisters Vandine, Myrtle Miller and May McGhan. Little did we know that the great-grandson of Sister Vandine would be a student at Columbia Christian College. Today his office is eight blocks from the college, and Bernie Supplee is our auditor, married to an elder's daughter, Peggy Kennedy.

Albany, Oregon — New Base of Operations

Our phone rang one night and it was Clyde Teel, an Albany business man, wanting us to move to a new and promising work there. (They had heard me lecture at Salem, Oregon.) They had about forty members with some fine talent among them. We accepted the challenge. Some of the leading men were Willard Bradley, Edward Walton and Theophilus Williams. The only full-time preacher in Oregon at the time was H.R. Thornhill in Salem, Oregon.

George Pepperdine continued our support at seventy-five dollars a month. We were moved and ready to go to work by September, 1941. December came and World War II broke out. George Pepperdine lost his fortunes in China, and our support was gone over night. It was time to make tents. The Presbyterian church advertised for a janitor at fifty dollars a month, and I took the job. When you take a job like that you have to have a sense of humor. I would tell my brethren, "I built a fire under the Presbyterians at 7 a.m. and I will build one under you at 11 a.m." Other janitorial jobs opened at the First National Bank, Western Union and Sears. Men were being called up for military service and work was plentiful. Families began moving to Oregon from Oklahoma, Texas and other states for defense contracts. Sammie's step-father died, and Mother Lacy and Edna Lea moved to Oregon, along with my parents, three sisters and one brother.

Window washers were in great demand. Mother Lacy, Edna Lea and my sisters went to work for me and when we would be out washing windows at the bank or Sears, people would stop and solicit our services on windows. The banker advised me to go to the court house and get a franchise on window washing, and this became another challenge in tent making.

My evangelistic work took me back to San Antonio, Texas, and besides the good we did in the meeting, we met Jim and Zoe Judge. Jim wanted to move to Oregon and work. I gave them both a job with the window washing

51

business. In fact, I named it after him, "J.J. Window Cleaners." The work was so demanding we also employed her mother and daddy, Bro. and Sis. Billy Klingman. He was one of the finest song leaders in the church. In Texas he was known as "The Sweet Singer of Israel." These people were a blessing to the work. At this time I was also in a position to answer calls for revivals, and Bro. Judge and Mother Lacy were responsible for my secular work.

The call came to start the work in Corvallis, Oregon. Two families were driving across the Willamette River to services in Albany — the Bewley and Copeland families. The summer of 1942 we were in a gospel meeting in Altus, Oklahoma, and an elder, George Starks, Manager of J.C. Penney Co., said, "I have an uncle living in Corvallis, Oregon, who is not a Christian, Mr. Jenkins. He is a brick layer. Please, try to reach him before it is too late." That fall we rented the I.O.O.F. Hall and held a gospel meeting. The attendance was great and Mr. Jenkins came. Several were baptized, including this fine man. We phoned Bro. Starks, and the church in Altus, Oklahoma, agreed to support a preacher to move into Corvallis. I had met Albert H. Smith, minister at Southside in Lubbock, Texas, who wanted to go west. On January 1, 1943, Bro. Smith arrived. He brought funds for a daily broadcast on the local radio station. The church bought a dwelling, remodeled it, and great things began to happen in that city. I made many visits to Corvallis to encourage the work. Brother Jenkins told me he had wanted to live long enough to lay the brick on a new building for the church. (He was seventy-two years old when he spoke to me about it.) Ten years later he laid the brick, and Albert H. Smith carried the mud.

I visited the Bewley family. They lived in Monroe, Oregon, and attended church in Corvallis. I would go to the woods and watch Bro. Bewley and his sons, especially Earl, as they logged with teams. It was a beautiful sight, especially to those who know horses and the woods. Earl courted and married my sister, Grace. He has served as an elder in Corvallis and Salem for many years, and together they have been faithful supporters of Columbia Christian College. Grace renders unselfish service to cancer victims, and they have raised a fine family of four children.

The call came again from Wallowa, Oregon. Bro. C.L. Fallwell had gone to La Grande, Oregon, and bought a vacant Nazarene building and was ready to organize the church in that busy, little city. We drove over to look at the possibilities. We bought a La Grande newspaper. Driving out of town, Sammie read the want-ads. Before her eyes was an ad for members of the Lord's church. The contact address was Swenney Shoe Repair Shop. We drove back to La Grande, looked up the shop and found Brother and Sister Sweeney from Pampa, Texas. I recall her words as though they were spoken today, "See there Daddy, I told you it would pay to put the ad in the paper." Excitement filled the air as we told of our plans to start the church with a gospel meeting.

Bro. Fallwell contacted C.B. Shropshire, minister of the Central church in Portland. Shropshire had moved there from Farmersville, Texas. He was an excellent song leader and preacher. He and I agreed to go to La Grande for a thirty-day meeting.

Again, I was able to buy daily radio time in La Grande and send the bill to Bro. Graham in San Antonio, Texas. Brethren came long distances to encourage the meeting. After a broadcast at the station, Mr. George Archer, minister of the Methodist church, was waiting in the lobby to talk to me. His members were pressing him on the subject of baptism. He had drawn up a proposition: "Resolved that the scriptures teach that baptism is by immersion, sprinkling and pouring as the three modes of baptism." George Archer, affirm; Claude A. Guild, deny. I phoned Sammie to send me my Greek Bible and my Methodist Discipline. With the date set, we canceled four nights of the meeting and got

53

down to serious business with the Methodists. In the meantime, we were announcing the debate on our broadcast. Bus loads of people came from Union Gap, Baker and Wallowa. Some of the people could not get in the building. There were three great nights, but on the fourth night Mr. Archer made his first constructive speech, pulled on his four-buckle overshoes and left without making his rebuttal speech. He left without even speaking to his Methodist people, and they were alarmed and ashamed. When they heard what the Bible taught concerning baptism, several individuals were baptized, and the church was begun in Baker.

Other churches were springing up. A few brethren met in Walla Walla, Washington. They planned a great meeting with several preachers taking part. They were Charles Andrews, Reginold Rogers, C.B. (Ben) Shropshire and L.D. Webb. Webb had just moved to the Central church in Portland, Oregon, to help C.B.Shropsire. These services were held in a Pentecostal building that had sleeping quarters upstairs. During the next year we established the church in Dallas, Oregon.

All this time the church in Albany was growing. We bought a store building and because of its growth we had to enlarge it three times. We had a radio program in Albany and during the construction of an Adventist school building, we explained that if people enrolled their children there, they would soon refuse to eat pork and then they would not want to go to Sunday school but attend Sabbath school instead.

During a Sunday morning service, the invitation was extended and a fine looking, bald man of about sixty came forward. He would not sit down but introduced himself as E. F. Thorp from Bono, Arkansas. He stated that he came from Arkansas to Albany to debate the Sabbath issue with me. He asked if I knew Bynum Black, John Fry or Joe Blue. He related how he had met all of them in debate, and I knew they were three of our finest preachers in Arkansas. He handed

54

me the propositions, and that was the end of the worship service that Sunday morning. He affirmed, "The scriptures teach that the Seventh day is the Sabbath of the Lord, has never been abolished by divine authority and must be kept in the Christian age." I was to affirm, "The scriptures teach that the first day of the week is enjoined upon Christians as a day of worship in this Christian dispensation."

Plans were made and the dates set for the debate. I needed a moderator and I had heard Will M. Thompson, Oklahoma City, Oklahoma, moderate for Foy E. Wallace, Jr., against Webber. I phoned him and he was willing to come. When he arrived, I immediately tried to get Bro. Thompson to debate him because he was Thorp's age. Thompson's reply was a classic, "Son, remember, young men are made for battle, older men are made for counsel. I'll load the shots and you fire them."

The day arrived. The editor of Signs of the Times was present, along with Mennonites, Catholics and our brethren from long distances. The best shot Thompson loaded was to be used to expose the two-law theory. (Adventists divide the Old Testament into two laws: the cermonial with circumcision and offerings and the great moral law, which consists of the ten commandments.) Thorp contended that when Paul said, "The law was nailed to the cross" (Colossians 2:14), he was speaking of the ceremonial law. At that point Bro. Thompson had me make a ham sandwich with all the trimmings. He rehearsed this well with me. I was to present it to Thorp, and he would have only two choices. He could refuse to eat it, but then he would have to find the prohibition for eating pork in the ten commandments. Of course, it is forbidden in Leviticus 11:7, and, according to Thorp, that is the ceremonial law. His other choice was to eat it. If he did, he would keep his proposition but lose his people, because they had been taught not to eat it. The sandwich became a great thorn in his flesh. Thompson further coached me not to go to new material until he resolved the sandwich issue. The debate ended after seven days, and the people saw Adventism fail because the law of the Old Testament is one covenant and not two (Romans 7:1-4; II Corinthians 3:5-11, Galatians 4:21-31).

Thorp died thirty days after the debate, and I thought I was going to die from exhaustion. I had borrowed a book from Bro. Joe Blue, Monk on Adventism, to prepare for the debate. Two weeks after the debate I got a letter from Brother Blue, and it had one sentence in it: "Dear Brother Guild, do not allow me to accuse you of being a book keeper," signed, Joe Blue. Needless to say, I returned it immediately.

After six months Frank Walker of Colorado wrote and said, "Thorp did not satisfy our people in the debate. I want to give satisfaction with a fourteen-night debate. We will use the same propositions." Ector R. Watson, minister in Vancouver, Washington, served this time as my moderator. We followed the same plan as before. When we came to the place for the presentation of the sandwich, Walker couldn't do any more with it than Thorp. We even exhorted him. "The editor of Signs of the Times is sitting in the audience, and he will meet you in the shadows tonight and ask you why you didn't do something with that sandwich." Walker went seven nights and announced that his wife was deathly ill and he would have to quit the debate. It spelled complete victory for the truth, and we baptized thirty-three people following the debate.

Roseburg was the next Oregon city on our list for evangelism. Ben Shropshire and I teamed again to make the great tent meeting in Roseburg a success. It was a very stormy day when we raised the tent. A Pentecostal preacher brought his three sons to help raise it and spread the sawdust on the floor.

We also teamed in Baker, Oregon, for another gospel meeting. Fallwell had bought a building there and was

56

remodeling it to make it suitable for the meeting. A fellow came by and saw Fallwell installing a baptistry. He had never seen one and asked a lot of questions. He concluded by saying, "But how do you know you will need it?" Fallwell replied, "Claude Guild is coming to sow the seed of the Kingdom, and you can be sure the seed will sprout and grow and there will be baptisms."

The Albany church invited L.D. Webb to conduct a meeting and asked him to mail the topics so they could advertise his coming. He was too busy to mail them and told me to just put down whatever I wanted, and he would preach on them. Well, the Christian church had just changed its name to the Church of Christ, hence, one of the subjects was, "Why the Christian church has changed its name in Albany." Webb did a good job and pointed out the things that had divided the once united body — instrumental music, the missionary society, and modernism in their schools and colleges. As a result, they came to hear Webb. In response to his preaching, the Christian church preacher, Irvin Harris, and one of their elders, Bro. Orville Phillips, took their stand with us.

By this time a few families were calling from McMinnville, Oregon, to get the work started there. Harris needed work, and I was making enough in my business to donate to the church a salary for him for three weeks. He joined me in a meeting in the I.O.O.F Hall. Great response came, including the obedience of a Casey family. I had been to Texas and learned in a meeting at Anson that they wanted to support a man on the field. I phoned them about Bro. Harris and and the church in McMinnville. They secured assistance from Hamlin, Texas, the two congregations underwrote Harris, and he stayed in McMinnville.

World War II was drawing to a close and a few families wanted to start a congregation in Independence, Oregon, and we started in the Professional Women's Club building. Word came that the war was over and the city had

57

a parade. I had speakers on my car that I used to advertise the gospel meeting in Independence and to preach in the bean, berry and hop fields. Therefore, I joined the parade and invited everyone to come and celebrate properly the end of the war with the church of Christ at the Women's Club building. We couldn't get all the people in the building, and we preached the gospel to them.

Other great families came to Albany, including Jesse Holland and his son, Don Holland and his family. The Colberts, more members of the Bradley family, Nig Henry and A.J. Carrol obeyed the gospel. (A.J. Carrol married my sister, Neaoma, and became my brother-in-law.)

During our years in Albany, Oregon, two wonderful children were born to us. Cheryl Ann was born July 29, 1943. We have always said that she never walked but ran. She did begin to run at an early age and has been running ever since. She was bald the first eighteen months of her life, and we wondered if she would ever have any hair. Today she is a beautiful woman and is a graduate of Harding University and a fifth-grade teacher. Her husband, Dr. Gary Elliott, is president of Columbia Christian College. They have two wonderful children, Douglas and Heather. Dr. Elliott has great demands made of him to preach for churches all over the brotherhood.

On July 28, 1944, Claude Weldon (Sonny) was born into our family. (His sisters named him Sonny. He wanted to change it when he went to college, but it hasn't been possible.) Sonny has been a joy to us, like all his sisters, especially his early interest in the ministry. At seventeen years of age he made a trip to Tanzania, E. Africa, with eleven other college students from Ft. Worth Christian College and Abilene Christian College. They stayed six months and helped build Chimala Mission Hospital and did village evangelism and baptized more than one thousand people. Sonny received his A.A. from Ft. Worth Christian, his B.A. from Harding University and his M.Div. from Abilene Christian College. He put in nine years as a missionary in Kenya under the leadership of the Brookside church in Tulsa, Oklahoma. When he returned home we had finished seven years at Tigard, Oregon, and the brethren wanted him to be their minister. At this writing he has been with them eight years, and it is the second largest church in Oregon. He married Eunice Skelton, whose daddy, Walter Skelton, was my first Sunday school teacher in Caldwell, Idaho. Bro. Skelton served many churches in Idaho, Oregon, Washington and Hawaii as minister. Sonny and Eunice have three precious boys: Chris, Eric Timothy and Theron.

Chapter 4

THE CANADIAN CALL

The call of evangelism was great in our hearts as we had established a large number of new congregations in Idaho, Oregon and Washington. J.C. Bailey, then of Radville, Saskatchewan, wrote about the work in Vancouver, B.C. There was a small congregation at Sixth and Carolina Streets of perhaps fifty members. They had never had a minister to work locally with them, and Bailey persuaded us to look at that work. We visited Vancouver, and the prospects looked very good. At least they had a building.

Our move from Albany was tearful but pleasant, and our arrival in Vancouver was very revealing. We were there only a few weeks when we realized why they did not have a local preacher. (Altus, Okalahoma, accepted the total oversight and support of our work.) This little church was made up of brethren largely from the British Isles. They practiced mutual ministry in England, and the church in Vancouver practiced it as well. Therefore, it was very difficult for them to give up the pulpit to a full-time preacher. They would take forty-five minutes at the Lord's table and leave ten minutes for me to preach. There were, however, a number of converts, including Brother Bob and Sister Lil Beamer. Bob was a former R.C.M.P. (Royal Canadian Mounted Police). They were excited about the work of the church and helped in many, many ways.

I recall many pleasant days in Canada. One Sunday we announced a tour of gospel meetings in the

States and asked for the prayers of the congregation. The announcer said, "We want to wish Bro. and Sis. Guild good luck on their tour of duty in the States." Bro. Bruce, a very active man in his eighties and very spiritual, arose to a point of order. He stated, "I didn't hear Bro. Guild state that he was going to Las Vegas where games of luck are played. I do not believe our minister travels by luck or the zodiac. I would rather say, "His journeying mercies, Bro. Guild." This was a beautiful statement and a picture of this very spiritual man, which I recall with fondness.

One Lord's day we had a very moving morning service. We were in the assembly when the light fixtures began to swing, the benches began to rock as the earth moved, and we heard the sound of dishes breaking in the basement. Bro. Summerscales was presiding and sensed the problem and asked for prayers. We were having an earthquake. He led the prayer and it was marvelous. "Lord, as our building, our homes and our city shakes, along with the ground upon which they stand, give us the calmness of the sea when Jesus stilled it and give us a sense of security, knowing there couldn't be a better place in which to be than together in worship when things like this happen." He continued his prayer until everything was calm.

After two years in Vancouver, the call came through W.R. Smith, Vice President of Abilene Christian College, to go to Corsicana, Texas. We prayerfully considered leaving the mission field and decided to move to Texas. We felt gratified in our leaving that we were able to encourage the congregation in Vancouver to hire a full-time minister. The man who followed us in the pulpit, Bro. Marshall, stayed over twelve years.

Our work in Canada did not end when we moved to Texas. In subsequent years we were able to conduct a large number of meetings in Canada and lecutred at Western Christian College. We had great meetings in Moose Jaw, Regina, Radville, Prince Albert and Weyburn. Several years later, when I was working with Columbia Christian College in Portland, Oregon, I took a young student from Abilene Christian College, Dan Danner, with me to lead the singing for a summer in Canada. Dan was from Portland, Oregon, and the son of Curtis Danner, an elder in the Eastside church of Christ. It was a great summer, and all this activity was but a spin-off from our short stay in Vancouver, B.C.

The Challenge of Corsicana, Texas

God had a way to call us, after eight-and-one-half years, out of the field to work with an established church and enjoy the association of strong brethren. He knew we needed to be recharged spiritually and to rest from the ordeals of new fields and battles on the front line. W.R. Smith phoned us and invited us to come back to Texas and accept the work at Fifth Avenue in Corsicana. He made the total arrangements. We sold our home and shipped our hosehold effects by rail.

We were instructed to visit W.R. Smith before going to Corsicana. This was the order of our meeting with him. Smith stated, "You have been called to Corsicana to preach. There are several reasons. One, my mother-in-law, Sister Christian, lives in Rice, Texas, and attends the Fifth Avenue church in Corsicana. She deserves to hear the very best." He went on to explain that Fifth Avenue had had several preachers in nine years. These men included Leroy Brownlow, Frank Dunn, Dillard Thurman and J.L. Hines. There had to be a reason for this procession of preachers — one leaving the stage just as another was coming on the scene. I soon learned the reason. The church followed a pattern of putting a son in the eldership when his father died. But one time it didn't work. Roy Harrison was a deacon and treasurer. His father died, and Roy was not invited to the

63

eldership because he was not qualified. He continued, however, to run the church through the treasury. Preachers understood that elders were the stewards of the church, not the treasurer. But if they didn't preach sermons which pleased him, Roy would hold up their paychecks. It was no wonder they lost so many preachers.

My best day in Corsicana was when I recommended a solution to the eldership. They needed to appoint a new treasurer. They phoned Bro. Harrison and informed him that his signature would no longer be honored at the bank, and he was not to write any more checks for the church. Bro. Majors, a fine new convert who was in the insurance business, accepted the job, and order and peace came to the body in this Navarro County city.

We outgrew the building and made plans to start a new congregation in the North Beaton District. We secured a large tent, advertised and had a meeting. Prior to the meeting, I had lectured at the Riverside church of Christ in Ft. Worth, Texas. Their elders attended the tent meeting and invited me to move to Riverside to be their preacher. Sammie and I prayed about it and decided we would go to Ft. Worth. Why not go, because we had accomplished all that W.R. Smith had commissioned us to do in Corsicana. Claude Holcomb followed me to Corsicana and stayed twenty-eight years. The processional of preachers in that church was over, and God was working through the elder-ship again.

To conclude the Corsicana tenure, I also remember what W.R. Smith said about Navarro County, Texas. "You may not stick to the county, but the county will stick to you." There wasn't a pound of gravel in the county -- only black mud -- and his assessment was very correct. When Bro. Smith learned of our leaving, he wrote us the following letter:

October 27, 1948

Dear Brother Guild,

I rejoice to learn of the recent reconciliations among the brethren. I think it is very commendable for the congregation there to be in such excellent condition upon the eve of your leaving. I have confidence that your stay in Ft. Worth will be fruitful.

I realize the Ft. Worth church needs a man with a lot of "Spizerinctus" like you, but inasmuch as you put the Corsicana congregation in its present state of mind and willingness to pull together, it occurred that your best service could be rendered there. However, it may prove for the best in the long run.

We shall be looking forward to your visit on the campus during homecoming. Write me whenever I can be of service in any way.

Yours truly,

W.R. Smith, Vice President

Frank Dunn of Dallas, Texas, wrote a letter of encouragement during our time of adjustment and struggle in Corsicana, which meant a great deal to Sammie and me. It read:

Dear Claude:

You are doing a great work, Claude, and they all love you and appreciate you for it. I have not talked with one person from Corsicana who does not your efforts. That is very unusual for Corsicana. You are the only man who had ever been there who was able to do exactly what needed to be done.

Your Friend,. . . .Frank

It was a great day to receive from the elders at Fifth Avenue a letter of commendation as we made our plans to depart for our new work with the Riverside church of Christ in Ft. Worth:

Dear Brethren:

Although we sincerely regret losing Bro. Claude Guild, we are glad to recommend him to you as being one of the ablest ministers in the brotherhood. Too, we would be most ungrateful if we failed to recommend, equally as well, his good wife and family.

They are leaving here with the love and respect of what we sincerely believe is from every member of this congregation. They have done an excellent work among the young people. They are leaving of their own and your insistence. Peace and harmony prevail throughout the congregation; as you are well aware, that much depends upon the preacher in the preservation of peace. Bro. Guild well and capably fulfilled his obligation in that respect.

Naturally we feel hurt. We feel crippled, but our loss is your gain, and Bro. and Sis. Guild go with our sincere goodwill, respect and love.

In the name of the Master,
J.E. Thompson, W.F. Williamson, J.R. Hart and J.A. Sowell, elders

66

The struggles and victories in Corsicana are recorded in this volume to help other preachers know that they are not alone in their preaching problems, and when they are true to the Book, with prayer and patience, there is victory. We also want the bystander and members in the pews to know that preaching is not all fried chicken and a piece of cake.

One of the greatest things that happened to us in Corsicana was on December 6, 1947. Mary Sue, our baby, came to live with us. Sammie had a doctor that caused some suspicions on our part. My doctor, Dr. Logston, said if anything happened so that Sammie's doctor couldn't deliver the baby, he would be glad to do it. The day arrived, and we entered the hospital about 3:30 p.m. Sammie's doctor came, and he had been drinking and said the birth would not be for at least two hours. Before the two hours were over, Sammie was wheeled to the delivery, and the nurses said to me, "Get us a doctor, the baby is coming." I saw a nice-looking fellow coming down the hall and asked his name. He said, "Dr. Hammel, can I help you?" "Yes, my wife is having a baby, and Dr. Will was to have delivered her and he has not shown up." In a few minutes Dr. Hammel came out and said, "5:27 p.m. and it is a girl." I asked what I owed him, and he said, "Nothing, I'll take it out of Will's hide." We were never billed, and I have told Mary Sue if she never amounts to anything it is fine, because she didn't cost us anything from the beginning.

Oh, but what a joy to have this little girl. She has been a blessing to us. Every day has been a picnic to her. Sammie will allow me to say Mary Sue is a daddy's girl. Growing up, she liked to wash cars, mow the lawn, and caddy for me, especially when I would let her ride on the pull cart down the hills. Sammie had the privilege of being her teacher in the first grade. She married Hugh Galyean, and they had two fine boys, Hugh Adrian and Douglas Eliot.

67

Mary Sue attended Lubbock Christian College two years. After her husband graduated from Harding College and preached for a year in Shreveport, they joined us in our work in Australia. Hugh then took a job in Oxon Hill, Maryland, after which he accepted a preaching position in Pineville, Louisiana.

Hugh took training in Washington, D.C., with the State Troopers and is now in the F.B.I. Mary Sue lives in Portland with her two boys and is a medical assistant in a fine clinic. She still loves sports, people and especially her daddy.

Finally, the greatest preaching event in Corsicana came about through a murder trial held in Corsicana. William Ray, a soldier in Ft. Worth, Texas, was accused of raping a girl. A change of venue was granted, and the trial was held in Corsicana. Al Clyde, district attorney, was seeking re-election and unmercifully sought the death penalty. The jury granted it, and he was in the death cell thirty days. I was moved by the man, William Ray. I was given permission to preach to him every day for thirty days. During that time he wanted a shave and hair cut. I had three barbers in the congregation, but no one would help. I trusted him, entered his cell and shaved him and cut his hair. He was very appreciative and listened well to the story of the cross. He was ready to obey the gospel, and we had to get a court order from the judge to take him to the church building to complete his baptism. He rejoiced in his new relationship with Christ and his hope of resurrection. After he became a Christian, he gained fifteen pounds on jail food, simply because he had peace of mind.

After two years in Huntsville, Texas, he paid the capital price for his crime, but he remained appreciative for his relationship with the Lord up to the day he died. Neither his wife nor his children claimed his body, but a broken little mother from Vernon, Texas, claimed it and buried him in a

68

family plot. I am thankful we reached him with the gospel in time. The report of his baptism was reported through the Associated Press.

Chapter 5

GOD LEADS IN FORT WORTH, TEXAS

1949 was a great year for the Lord to take control again in our lives for missions. The Riverside church had built its new building and planned a lectureship. I do not know where they got my name or heard of me, but I was invited to speak. The house was full, and the assigned subject was "The Dangers of Indifference Toward Speculative Teachings." During the lecture, from the middle of the house, a very white-headed man stood up and shouted, "Say on, brother." Later, I learned he was a great pioneer preacher, Price Billingsley. From that lecture the elders sought me out in Corsicana, and we moved January 1, 1949.

An eldership can be a catalyst around which great things come to pass. God led us to a visionary and spiritual eldership: W.C. Sparkman, Carl Bradshaw, R.H. Banowsky, J.H. Tew, W.E. Stewart and H.B. Bruce. These men began a number of ministries that built the church locally, city-wide and around the world. They signed contracts for two radio programs, KCNC weekdays and KWBC Sunday mornings. We began reaching out. One man from out of state tuned in, heard the sermon on his car radio, drove to the building and requested baptism for the remission of sins. The membership was four hundred, with a Sunday morning attendance of about three hundred seventy-five.

The work jumped forward the first four months, and Riverside hired its first full-time secretary, Bobby Smith.

Radio correspondence, letters to visitors and a new bulletin format demanded the capable services of Sis. Smith.

The second ministry came in a challenge from W.R. Smith of Abilene Christian College and Reuel Lemmons of Clebourne, Texas. Reuel Lemmons presented the need for support for a missionary to South Africa, John Hardin. Later, Bro. Smith encouraged us to support a native Australian, Allan Flaxman, to return to his home country to preach the gospel. The offers were the same — five years at $5,000 a year, $20,000 per missionary or a gross expenditure of $50,000. The elders and deacons met. (Prior to this involvement Riverside had only given about $1,500 a year in missions.) Things began very poorly in the meeting. A deacon reminded the men we owed $99,000 on the building, and times could get bad and we could lose the building because of this mission work. He wanted them to remember he registered his protest. Elder W.C. Sparkman took the floor and said, "I have seen Riverside grow from a shotgun frame building to our new Austin stone building, and we are having weekly additions. I remember the nice things we bought for ourselves without objection: air conditioning, posturpedic pews, carpets and an elevated baptistry. This has gone on twenty-eight years for us, and we have done nothing for the mission field. I am not in favor of supporting either Hardin or Flaxman, but I want us, by faith, to accept the challenge of both of them. Our deacon brother may be right. We could lose this building, but, if it is because of mission work, here is what I will do. I will guarantee the checks for missions for five years with my company, S. & T. Supply Company." Imagine an elder putting his business on the line for mission work! God was present in that meeting and knew what was said and done.

After one year with our oversight of Flaxman and Hardin on the fields, Sparkman opened another store in Houston. He declared, "My new store in Houston made more money than the home store, and I am ready to sacrifice more of my business for more missionaries." During the next four years, Riverside grew at home from 400 members to 1,183. They accepted more mission challenges: J. Lee Roberts in France, Bro. Matthews in Maine and two native preachers in Mexico.

A third ministry that opened was a men's training class. This class was made up of grown men. Some were seasoned preachers; others were learning. F.L. Paisley, Tom Murray, Will Slater, Wade Banowsky, Thurman Still, Frank Summerour, Noble McKillip, Steve Patterson, and Dr. A.K. Roach were some of the first students. These men filled many pulpits around Ft. Worth and also served Riverside in my absence.

The fourth ministry at Riverside was the New Year's Eve singings. This was an event that attracted brotherhood attention. The church had hired a song leader, Bro. Foy Hall, something few churches were doing. He was responsible for these great singings. January 7, 1951, saw 1,500 in attendance. People came from ten states, and thirty-eight cities in Texas, and twenty-two congregations in Ft. Worth were represented. Choruses and quartets came, and our audiences and special numbers had to be served in shifts. By this time the membership had grown from 400 to 830, while regular contributions grew from $15,000 to $43,600.

The fifth ministry was a boys' training class on Saturdays. It would vex my soul to see kids lined up two blocks long to get in the Saturday show at Six Points, perhaps ten blocks from our property. The elders authorized us to have a class for boys on Saturday and follow the class with softball games. The enrollment was heavy. Among those enrolled were Bill Banowsky and Bill Knowles. We required memory verses. The above two young men challenged each other to memorize entire chapters of scripture.

There was a young man, Tommy Pettit, who looked longingly at the boys playing softball. He was a senior in high school and a Catholic. We invited him to play, but he would have to come to class. After three months he obeyed the gospel. In the next nine months he chose Harding College as his home away from home for college. He came to see me with a suitcase and Bible under his arm. It was Tuesday morning. He stated his good-byes and then said, "My parents are not in favor of this trip to Harding. Mother wouldn't give me sheets, pillow cases or clothes. Dad wouldn't give me any money. I am hitchhiking to Harding, and I know the Lord will find a way for me to complete my college education." I shared his story with the seventy-five ladies who met for ladies' Bible class. They gathered sheets, pillow cases, shirts, ties and the whole ball-of-wax and took up money. Most of it was on the campus waiting for him when he arrived. They mothered him through college, and Bro. L.W. Richardson got him a job with West Texas Electric Service when he finished his degree.

Other great things came from that training class. Twelve years later I received a letter from William S. Banowsky:

September 8, 1965

Dear Claude,

Thank you for your thoughtful letter. . . . Of course, you know that you have had more influence upon my decision to preach and my preaching style than any other man alive. When I was a boy you caught my fancy and lit a fire in my soul which has never gone out. I will be eternally grateful to you for that. May God bless you.

Sincerely,
Bill Banowsky,
Minister, Broadway church of Christ.

There was a sixth ministry, and fruit from it was abundant. The jail of Tarrant County opened an opportunity for us to preach on Sundays and study with the prisoners during the week. We accepted this challenge for three years, and it resulted in forty-three conversions. David Mastin was one convert that led to others. Melvin Harbinson was another. (We only worked on the floor of federal offenders.) Sully Montgomery was the county sheriff, and he would always escort us to the Riverside building for baptisms. Sully had been a professional prize fighter and an important personality in Ft. Worth. At the close of a baptismal service for prisoners, Sully pulled off his gun belt, took his cowboy boots off and said, "I want some of that," meaning baptism for the remission of sins. That put the icing on the cake for our jail work. But many people helped in the success of the program. One who made a significant contribution was L.W. Richardson.

Other conversions at the Riverside church were outstanding. I had a phone call from Bro. W.J. Braune, elder at Southside church of Christ. He related how his mother was widowed, worked in a laundry, and different neighbors took the children to various Sunday schools. He was carried to the church of Christ. His twin bother, O.B. Braune, was carried to the Assembly of God. W.J. was an elder in the church of Christ, and his twin was a minister in the Assemblies of God. He learned that I had been a Lutheran and encouraged me to go to his mother and teach her. I did and the day of her baptism arrived. We were told by Mother Braune to invite all her children. We did this. She was crippled and it was a little difficult to get her in the baptistry. Her son who was the minister in the Assembly of God church ran up to the baptistry, took off his shoes and helped get her into the water. All the children witnessed her obedience.

75

Every time I would see W.J. he would say, "Thank God, Bro. Guild, we got to Mother in time."

Peggy Selcer was Presbyterian and a friend of some of our members. Her mother died, and her minister was on vacation and unable to conduct the funeral. She was deeply hurt because it seemed that her mother was buried without proper circumstances. We visited her and gave her a copy of Charles R. Brewer's book, Be Not Dismayed. We invited her to ladies' class, and she came with excitement and learned readily. Her husband, Dick Selcer, was an American Airlines pilot. On Mother's Day she asked Dick to go to church with her at Riverside. He was offended and took the family to the Presbyterian church, where they had been absent for nearly a year. Before they could go to class, the pastor took them in the office, related how much they were behind on their tithes and wanted a check. Dick asked Peggy, "Where is that church where you have been going?" She told him again about Riverside, and he said, "Let's get down there right now."

We had studies with him and two neighbors, Dick Jones, a Lincoln Mercury dealer, and Frank Brooks, Assistant Manager at Swift and Company. On a Tuesday morning after the Monday study, Dick Selcer phoned and said he was ready, and he had talked to Dick Jones and he was ready. I was to talk to Frank and Evelyn Brooks. Sammie and I went over and had breakfast with them, and that day three new families were baptized into Christ: Selcers, Jones and Brooks.

While we are on conversions, the list would be incomplete without mentioning the conversion of Mr. Sam Jones. The elders hired this black man to do the janitor work. He had great experience, having only held two jobs in his lifetime. (He was a porter on the Southern Pacific and a caretaker for an insurance company in Cowtown. He was a Methodist.) My secretary, Mae Lewis, and I immediately began teaching Sam. Mae was very kind and patient with him. He responded well to the things we said. However, Sam would forget instructions. He was not to spray my office for cockroaches or other insects on days I would be in the office. (His sprays caused me to have asthma.) Sam often forgot. One time I told him if I ever baptized him, I would hold him under the water, until the bubbles came up, for forgetting about spraying my office.

Two years passed and one Sunday night we offered the invitation and from the balcony came Sam Jones. He was crying and I asked him, "Sam, have you come to obey the gospel?" He said, "Brother Guild, I have wanted to obey the gospel so long I have threatened to go up there and jump in by myself." After his confession he requested that Bro. Lawrence Richardson baptize him. In the changing rooms he told Bro. Richardson why he asked for him and related how I had told him I would hold him under the water. He was a great Christian, and his little girl, Posqualie, spent many days at our place playing with Mary Sue.

The spirit of missions spread from Riverside even more in the U.S.A. Bro. Everett and his wife were very faithful members. He worked on the Rock Island Railroad. He had a divisional point in Herrington, Kansas, and lamented many times about not having a church there. He brought it to the elders, and they licensed me to go with other workers and start the church in that little city. We did this, and it made a place for Bro. Everett to worship away from home. My song leader for several years at Riverside was Odell Bramlett. He lived in Azel, Texas. There was no church there. A mission thrust was planned by the church. They had plenty of benches and lights for outdoor meetings. We trucked them to Azel, did a lot of door knocking and advertising. The congregation at Riverside came en masse. During the meeting Bro. Homer Steadman attended, a man who had started many churches in the Ft. Worth area and was mission minded, drove a large truck with a load of lumber into the field where the meeting was held and asked to say something. He declared, "We need a church in Azel and to add to the efforts of Riverside I want to give the first load of lumber for the new building." That meeting resulted in a congregation, building and a great church in Azel. The date for the beginning of the church in Azel was May 23, 1954.

Riverside reached out to Alex Humphries in Rock Springs, Wyoming, and helped with his support and also supported Bro. E.R. Davis in Houlton, Maine. They donated $1,950.50 to a new work in Italy by the Paden brothers. Weldon B. Bennett, supported by Union Avenue church of Christ in Germany, was forced to sell his car to have furlough money for his family. Before they returned, he had a meeting with us at Riverside, and the elders thought he could not do his work properly without a car. On the last night of the meeting we wanted to take up a large enough contribution to buy him an automobile. We passed the plates and lacked a few hundred dollars. I know there are a lot of things said about my fund raising, and this is the only time we said, "Lock the doors; no one is leaving until we get enough for the car for a missionary." We passed the plates again and went over the top. Bro. Bennett has always appreciated that gift. (He came home five years later and finished his ministry as a member of the faculty at Abilene Christian College.)

By the spring of 1952, the elders saw we could not house the membership in our building. We had grown to 1,183 members, and children were invited to sit on the pulpit floor around me to make room for adults. We ran a series of evangelistic services that ran two years and only had two Sundays when there were no baptisms. In fact, they came so regularly, Larry Costlow, little three-year-old son of

Brooks and Ella Mae, cried dreadfully loud on one of our "dry" Sundays, and Ella Mae took him out. I spoke to her in the foyer, and she said he was crying because, "I wanted to see Uncle Claude in the water."

The elders laid down the ground rules for a new congregation. The Riverside elders would select the leadership for the new congregation, they would support the exodus and they would give the new work its blessing. Brethren Bill Burlison, Wade Banowsky, Frank Allen and T.L. Cannon were appointed trustees, and, after the land was bought on 28th Avenue, the groundbreaking was held October 5, 1952. The contractor was selected, a new convert, Seth Castleberry. (We had baptized his children first, Joan and Jerry. Later we could really talk to Seth when we personally helped him unload a carload of cement one night. After that he knew preachers were human. We took him and his good wife, Clada, and saw them born into the Kingdom.) Riverside financed the building with seating for 300 people and furnished the song books, Bibles and communion service. Don H. Morris, President of Abilene Christian College, was the speaker at the dedication. Three hundred members chose to go with the new work, and the transition was beautiful. Plans were made for the building to be built with volunteer labor. Men and women from Riverside worked night and day. We completed it with the additional expenditure of $52,280. Riverside's mission budget grew from $1,500 in 1948 to $47,250 in 1952.

L.D. Webb, evangelist from Portland, Oregon, came for a meeting in 1953. He did a fine job of preaching but also had long talks with Sammie and me to come to Portland to build a new congregation on the east side and to help with Columbia Bible School. Our interest grew and by early 1954 we made the decision to go to Portland. We took it up with the elders and told them we needed five months to find our support. In the same meeting I resigned, and Riverside hired me to go to Portland.

Before leaving Riverside we recall among the hundreds that came to obey the gospel, two beautiful people. D'Esta Lea, our oldest daughter, was baptized on Easter in 1952, and one Sunday while I was away, Carl Bradshaw, an elder in that great Riverside church, baptized Sonny into Christ. We also got to see the Eastridge and Riverside churches grow until they joined with Diamond Hill and formed a new and beautiful work that continues to this day, namely, the Midtown church of Christ.

Chapter 6

PORTLAND, OREGON, FOR THE FIRST TIME

Farewells were spoken at Riverside, and June 1, 1954, we started a new work in Portland and Columbia Bible School. We arrived with a letter from the elders at Riverside which said:

Greetings to whom this may come:

This will recommend to your fellowship and confidence, our Bro. Claude A. Guild, who has been local, full-time minister with this congregation for five years.

We are sending him to the Northwest with our blessing and support. He has proven to be an able and zealous worker, having accomplished for this congregation more than any who have ever served here. We would gladly have him remain but he feels bound in the Spirit to go into more needy fields and we are not selfish enough to restrain him. We are therefore underwriting his personal support and recommending him to you as a man of faith, zeal and deep conviction, well qualified to undertake the carrying of the pure gospel to those who have not heard; to build up congregations, teaching them the Lord's methods of operation and for raising funds for the support of Columbia Bible School.

With prayer for his success and your support, we are:

Yours in the faith, the Elders:

R.H. Banowsky, Carl Bradshaw, Glen Holden, W.C. Sparkman, W.E. Stewart, and J.H. Tew

Columbia Bible School had started in 1947 in the old Central church of Christ building at 7th and Hassalo in Portland. Thirteen acres of land were purchased at 90th and N.E. Glisan where an auditorium, four classrooms and a broom closet were built, and a new congregation was begun in the school building by the time we arrived. We immediately joined ourselves to the work. The Board of Trustees elected me Vice President of the school, and the elders of the Eastside church of Christ — Walter Burkett, Earl Smith, Chester Kennedy and Bert Claspill — invited me to share the pulpit with Bro. L.D. Webb.

The Eastside church was begun in June, 1953. During the first year they ordained four elders: Earl Smith, Chester Kennedy, Bert Claspill and Walter Burkett. There was a small auditorium in the new school plant in which the church met for worship. A rent adjuster was hired to measure the square footage, electrical outlets, office space and other details, and he determined the rent to be paid by the church to the school. It was $200.00 a month.

The work took on immediate growth. There were fifty-one additions the first three months of 1954. Brother Webb and I would alternate on tours in the Southland for meetings and for raising funds for the school. Our meetings yielded three hundred seventy-three responses, and seventy-three of them were baptisms. Bro. Webb was in meetings in Sulphur Springs, Oklahoma; Peak and Eastside in Dallas, Texas; Hood River, Oregon; Sunnyside,

82

Washington; and Buena Park, California. My meetings took me to Prineville, Madras and Bend, Oregon; Yakima and Goldendale, Washington; Pleasant Grove in Dallas; Calmont and Rosemont in Ft. Worth; Pleasanton Grove, Texas; Holdenville, Oklahoma; Pueblo, Colorado and Agnes, Oregon.

The meeting in Agnes was really different. A number of brethren had gone down on the Rogue River to log out a section of timber. C.H. George was in charge of the enterprise. Walter Burkett, Chet Haven, Bill Powell and other Christians worked for him. They had built temporary shacks, meeting hall and kitchen. Brother Burkett wrote me to come for a meeting and promised he would let me fish during the day, if I would preach for them ten days in a meeting. He said, "We have a guest house for you right behind our cabin." We hurried to Agnes to preach. We discovered the guest house was a tent Burkett had put up for us, and it was great. He ran the ferry for the logging trucks on the river and when they were not waiting, Walter Burkett fished with us on the Rogue River. Many of the Indians in the area attended the meeting, along with other local residents. There were four baptisms. More came from that meeting, too.

Webb had pointed out to me that we needed twelve venetian blinds for the classroom windows. During the last Sunday afternoon of the meeting I visited the loggers' camp. I told them our needs — it would take fifty-five dollars to install a blind, and we needed twelve of them. Everyone responded to our appeal. We took up thirteen checks. I told them that night, "You loggers have ruined me. We only needed twelve blinds, but you gave me thirteen checks. Therefore, we will have to go home and make another window to put up another blind."

Burkett found some boys along the river who could go to high school, but fished and played until they were old enough to work in the woods. He talked two families into letting him have two fine boys to go to Columbia Bible School. They were Gene Brock and John McCrey. He took them down river and loaded up his Jeep and headed for Portland. Noon came and Walter said, "We'll stop in the next town and eat lunch." Neither boy had eaten at a cafe. They decided to just watch Walter and order whatever he ordered. The waitress came to their table and Walter said, "Bring me a menu." John said, "Bring me one, too." Gene said, "Bring me one and put catsup on mine." These boys did fine in school, and today, thirty-five years later, many of their families are in the Portland area and are faithful members of the body of Christ.

The growth at Eastside can be credited to a great extent to the visiting men who held gospel meetings for us or conducted special series of lessons. Among those who were with us were Otis Gatewood, Frank Dunn, Leroy Brownlow, Abe Lincoln, Paul Williams, Hugh Shira, Walter H. Adams and Don H. Morris. As we added new men to our staff and faculty, they were a great strength to the work. Holland L. Boring, Sr. was our first dean and was head of the music division. Holland L. Boring, Jr. was one of our coaches and Don H. Boring served on the faculty. The Borings were responsible for getting a Northwest singing normal started and most of the time it was conducted on campus. Choice Bryant and J.C. Cliffard were added to the teaching staff of the normal. Earl Butcher was added to our teaching staff, and he and the Borings were responsible for a lot of preaching for little churches in the Portland area.

July 11, 1955, the elders at Eastside selected a building committee. They chose the lots next to the academy building because the bus turnaround was on the corner of 90th and Glisan, and anybody could come from any place in the Portland area to the church or the school. January 8, 1956, $50,000 was raised to pay for the lots. Generous contributions were made toward the land by Eastside members, and funds were raised throughout the country.

August, 1956, we had $17,300 in our building fund and on February 27, 1957, we had the first meeting with our architect, Charles Brummett. December 20, 1957, the plans for the building were approved.

Evangelism blossomed in the Northwest through the teamwork of Guild and Webb. The Westside church was begun November 18, 1956, in a rented hall on Silvan and Canyon Rd., with thirty-three people present and a contribution of $96.00. Connard Estes, teacher at Columbia Bible School, did the preaching and Don Boring led the singing. By April 7, 1957, the church was begun in Woodburn, Oregon, with Choice Bryant preaching. They met in the armory building and there were forty-one present.

Meanwhile, meetings were going strong for L.D. and me. I held three meetings with two hundred seven responses, twenty-seven of which were baptisms. (The responses were as follows: Eastside in Tulsa, with 78 restored and 16 baptisms; North Houston with 69 responses and 7 baptisms; 23rd and Grace in Wichita Falls, Texas, with 60 responses, including 4 baptisms.) We were also pressed into a meeting in Pendleton, Oregon. Sometimes brethren wonder what a preacher is paid in all these meetings. Let me state here that I have been in evangelistic work fifty-four years and from the first meeting to the last there have been less than ten churches that have made advance arrangements for pay. You hold the meeting, they pay you and you take it and learn to like it and not question the logic. I do not know of a plumber, electrician or carpenter or any other tradesman that works under these arrangements. I have never set a price on my preaching, but it is unfair and unprofessional to expect ministers to spend their own money for transportation, and sometimes for advertising, and then spend their time in preparation and their energies during the meeting and be given a token for their travel expenses.

85

To illustrate this point, I helped in a meeting in a city in Oregon where they had a local preacher (he should, by the way, be consulted about these matters) and there were many tradesmen in the congregation. There were three men trucking logs. I ate in their homes, and they boasted that they could clear one hundred dollars a day driving logging trucks. I drove fifteen hundred miles to the meeting, doing personal work and going to the services. (They had me stay in a home fifteen miles from town.) The last night of the meeting we baptized four souls into Christ. There were more baptisms that week than they had witnessed in a long time. They came to me like I was Danny White, quarterback for the Dallas Cowboys, and wanted me to come back the same time next year. After everyone had left, the lone treasurer handed me an envelope, which was sealed. Then he turned off the lights and went to his car and I went to mine. I turned on the dome light in the car and found in the envelope a check for $25.00. That was pay for a two-Sunday meeting, 1,500 miles on my car and the wear and tear both on me and my automobile. If the three brothers had not boasted of making a hundred dollars a day, it would have been a different ball game. Let me suggest — write the evangelist, state what you can pay and make this arrangement before he comes to town. It will be handled with greater honor and dignity than sealing a $25.00 check in an envelope and leaving him in the dark to open it and go home underpaid.

During that 1956-57 period I also conducted meetings in Corvallis, Oregon; University Church in Denver, Colorado; Montana Street in El Paso, Texas; Vernon, Texas; Coos Bay, Oregon; Moose Jaw and Regina, Sask., Canada; Granger and Pasco, Washington; Riverside in Fort Worth, Texas; and Seminole and Holdenville, Oklahoma. Bro. Webb held great meetings in Yreka, California, with his son, David, leading the singing and there were eight baptisms and three restorations. Grants Pass, Oregon, was a great meeting for him with fifteen baptisms; Goldendale, Washington, had four baptisms; and Corvallis, Oregon, had thirteen baptisms and six restorations.

The work at Eastside was prospering with great conversions. Ferd Powell, former instrumental church of Christ preacher, took his stand with us and did a great ministry. He would ride the buses and pass out literature. He would also preach in my absence. We built a bus stop booth in the turnaround, put lights in it from our building and tract racks. Brother Powell kept it stocked and used it as a point of contact with people who came to ride the buses.

Another great conversion was reaching the Elmer Maxwell household. I had been to Coos Bay, Oregon, for a gospel meeting and Sister George Button spoke to me about reaching her sister, Edna Maxwell, in Portland. She had doubts about their interest in church but wanted us to see about putting the children in Sunday school. Dudley Collins, a deacon in the Eastside church, toured with me for three days to see what a preacher did during the week. Among other calls we made, we called on Elmer and Edna Maxwell. The reception was cordial from the beginning. The commitment was made to bring their children to Bible school, and to our surprise Elmer and Edna enrolled also. They came faithfully, studied with us, and, on March 17, 1957, they obeyed the gospel. They grew well and fast. Elmer was made a deacon in 1959 and served six years. He was then ordained into the eldership and served until May, 1987, making a total of twenty-five years in an ordained office for this fine man. Edna became a secretary to Columbia Christian College and served eight years (1968-1976) and then served eleven years as registrar of the college. Both of them are now working very hard with the Asian congregation that meets in Eastside's basement.

Another family that had a unique conversion was Bro. and Sis. Tant Harmon. Mr. Harmon came to church and inquired about answers to some questions he had. (He had been watching our T.V. program.) I visited his home and my first question was, "Where did you get the name 'Tant'?" He related that his folks were members of the church in Western Oklahoma. The depression years drove him west to find another way to live rather than on a sandy farm in Mangum, Oklahoma. He landed in Salt Lake City, Utah, completed his business college course and took work in Salt Lake City. There he met and married a Mormon girl. They had a daughter eight years old, and the Mormons were going to baptize her and Tant, with a long list of the dead to be baptized with them. Mr. Harmon objected to this arrangement. He suggested to his wife, "Let's go to my family church and see what they teach." After several studies we baptized both Tant and his wife into Christ. Oh, yes, he was named by his parents after a well-known preacher in the church, J.D. Tant. By this time he owned an auditing business on 29th and N.E. Sandy and became very helpful to Columbia Bible School and useful in the church. One of the delights of my life was to stop in Mangum, Oklahoma, visit his people and tell them that Tant was baptized into Christ, along with his wife, and was busy in the kingdom.

James Murray is another name worth mentioning in this special list of wonderful converts. James was a cement contractor. His wife was a member at Eastside, and James came with her all the time. We needed steps poured for our new church building. Sometimes it was Columbia Bible School or the college that needed cement jobs, and Mr. Murray was always there to do a good job and never billed any of us for his work. He was too good to miss heaven.

One day I went early to see Mr. Murray. He was snapping beans. I asked him what he would be doing that morning. He replied, "How about me taking Mary to work at Penney's first?" I told him that would be fine. He thought I had another job for him. I told him why I had come. I wanted him to get a bundle of clothes, come by the building after he took Mary to work and be baptized. His word was always good and he said he would come by. Sure enough, in about an hour James came with his bundle of clothes, and I baptized him. He wept after his baptism and told me he was ashamed to cry, but it was the happiest day in his life. I said, "James, why did you wait so long to obey the gospel?" He said, "Until this morning, no one had asked me." He continued to serve the Lord, even bought a home close to the building so when they got older they could always get to church.

It would be a mistake not to mention that Cheryl Ann was baptized in 1955 and Mary Sue in 1959 — both in the school auditorium with the make-shift baptistry under the stage. L.D. Webb baptized Cheryl Ann, and I baptized Mary Sue. These great girls have remained true to their calling in Christ Jesus, along with all our other children and their children.

Meanwhile, Eastside elders appointed Charles Brummitt as architect of our new building at Eastside on December 20, 1957. January 9, 1979, the plans were approved and the groundbreaking was set for April, 19, 1959. It was not as exciting as we had planned. During this time anti-cooperation had spread throughout the Northwest and had divided the brethren and the churches. The very Sunday we planned our groundbreaking, a few members, persuaded by a roving preacher that we had used coopera- tive funds to build the building, announced they were leaving and were starting a new work at N.E. 160th in Portland. Bill Powell, Sr. announced it and fired a shot as good as the one in Texas which is remembered as "Remember the Alamo." Bill's call was, "Let's see you build a Teepee without us." He was from Oklahoma and it was a fitting image. We went ahead with the groundbreaking and announced our bond sale. Dennis Moss, new convert from the Advent Christian church, bought the first bond. The elders asked me to keep ahead of the carpenters, and we went to work.

Forrest H. Anderson, Oregon City, began digging the basement on May 15, 1959. He was a great workman. Our costs would have been much more if he had not been so generous. We had raised $50,000 in cash, and with $170,000 in bonds the building would be built with all volunteer labor. The bonds bore 5 1/2% interest. Since it was the first bond issue among churches of Christ in the Northwest, they went very well. By the spring of 1960 they were all sold except $60,000. I went to Texas to sell the balance. Among those who bought was Billy Sol Estes. I knew him as a boy in Clyde, Texas. I lacked $6,000 when I learned that our first grandson, Stuart Mark Love, was born in Abilene, Texas. We sent to see him and while visiting Stuart and D'Esta, I thought of Dr. John Paul Gibson, M.D., who had always been good to me. I saw him, and he took the last $6,000. It was a great day. The brethren continued working. In fact, they worked sixteen months, every Saturday but two, and the ladies fixed lunch for them continuously. We knew how to start, erect and complete a "teepee" in Oregon.

Chapter 7

COLUMBIA CHRISTIAN COLLEGE
IS ESTABLISHED

September 3, 1956, was a historical day for the Northwest. The Board of Trustees for the school met and made plans to establish a junior college. Archie Warren, minister from Longview, Washington, made an outstanding address as to the needs for a Christian college in the great Northwest. The Board of Trustees gave license to the administration to proceed with their plans. (The trustees were Earl D. Smith, Sewell Magnani, Harold Hamstreet, Raymond Winters and Chester Havens, Portland; Bill Wells, Hood River; H.O. Martin, Medford; Otis Marshall, Kenneth McEwen and Walter S. Burkett, Eugene; E.J. Berry, Salem; Bill McCoy and Thurman Ward, Goldendale, Washington.)

Prior to the above date, the school had an auditorium, four classrooms and a large broom closet. We immediately moved to the campus an old granary-like surplus building Bro. Walter Burkett found for us, and it was known as "Burkett Hall." Four grades were taught in this hall, and the rest of the grades, along with high school, operated in the other classrooms and auditorium with curtains. L.D. Webb, Holland Boring, Sr. and I had our offices in the broom closet.

The time had arrived to build more classrooms. An addition of 330 X 65 feet was arranged, and the call went out for funds to erect the structure. I had helped in a meeting in Corvallis, Oregon, and a Bro. Raymond Taylor from Oklahoma was restored in that meeting. The next Sunday he made a contribution of $2,500 to the church, a sign of genuine repentance for the years he had been out of Christ. I learned he brought a sawmill on the back of a truck from Oklahoma and was running Taylors Sawmill in Lobster Valley. He related how he would saw up a load of lumber, take it to town, sell it and lease more acres of trees at five cents an acre. He told us to let him know what lumber we needed for our new addition and he would help us. One of the biggest orders was the dimensional beams, sixty-five feet long. He could and did saw them, but we had to find transportation. After calling several transport companies, Mitchell Transfer agreed to have flatbeds come by the mill and bring them to the school as a contribution. We had to agree to unload them at the college even if the trucks came at night. Sure enough, the trucks arrived at night and boarding students, along with board members and other brethren, came to the school and unloaded the lumber. Sewall Magnani, a fisherman in Alaska during the summer, was our lead carpenter, and the building was underway.

February 2, 1958, I had been invited to the Annual President's Conference in Nashville, Tennessee. (June 2, 1957, Bro. L.D. Webb resigned as President of the school and as minister of the Eastside church.) It was a time of great mourning and sorrow to all the church and school community, but we had to pick up the pieces and go forward. The Board of Trustees asked me to be acting president until a new man could be selected. The Board also borrowed money to send me to Nashville. At that meeting Bro. A.M. Burton, President of the American Life and Casualty Insurance Company, Nashville, Tennessee, had his eightieth birthday and wanted to give gifts rather than receive them. He gave each college represented $2,500 in shares in his insurance company. I waited until the next day to go to his home and thank him. On that day I told Bro. Burton that $2,500 would buy one month's postage for Bro. Don Morris at Abilene Christian College, but for us it would buy the nails and hardware for a building with twelve classrooms. After explaining what we were doing, he went to his home office, brought out three more certificates worth $7,500 and said, "Buy some windows, plumbing and electrical supplies for that building too." However, he swore me to secrecy around Nashville about the additional certificates. Well, there was great joy in Portland when we brought home the additional funds.

God sent us Bro. Bob Rowland from Alaska. He was a great staff person and became a greater influence in the school, as will be revealed later. On one occasion, when funds were very low and Bro. Rowland and I sat in my office working on a solution, I spotted a broom in the corner. I said, "Bob, let's staple a straw to each letter and say, 'This is the last straw.'" We did this. We sent a copy of the letter to Bro. B.C. Goodpasture, editor of <u>The Gospel Advocate</u>. He ran it on the back page of the <u>Advocate</u>. That letter brought us $80,000.

Teams were formed between teachers, students and friends of the school and great competition was created. Earl Butcher headed up one team and Karl Love headed the other. Some team members would come as early as daylight to put the roof on but especially to outdo the other team. An elder, Bert Claspill, ran the tar bucket and Earl Smith and Chet Kennedy were good carpenters. Bro. Kennedy worked at a plywood plant and got reject sheets of five-eight plywood for a dollar a sheet.

The building was weathered in and the inside was useable before it was totally finished. Ivan Weltzin, Goldendale, Washington, was a brick layer and out of work and loved the school. He came down and he and I were responsible for the brick that is on that building today. Weltzin stayed with the Danner family and was paid two dollars an hour. We hired Bro. Brackett, black minister at the Mallory church of Christ, who carried the mud for one dollar an hour. Ivan and I would not want a tape on all the brick work, but we struck all the joints, cleaned them with acid and now thirty-one years later the brick is still there, and the building is still a blessing. It has twelve classrooms and three offices with ample restrooms.

You might want to know what we did about commodes, wash basins and urinals in this building. By the time we were qualified to receive government surplus properties, a lot of plumbing was available through an agency in Walla Walla, Washington. With the proper papers I drove my 1951 Studebaker to Walla Walla. They tied my seat cushions on the top of the car and loaded me with three commodes, three wash basins and three urinals. We were blessed with Roscoe Lewis from Montana who could install all the fixtures with the expertise of a fine plumber.

The church and college were a great load to our family as I tried to sell $170,000 worth of bonds for Eastside church (which we did) and keep contributions coming for the college. By June 5, 1958, we had the dedication of the new church building with M. Norvel Young, President of Pepperdine College, as the speaker. We also had a new president for the college, T.H. Etheridge, Alpine, Texas. In appreciation for what we did, directing the college and soloing for Eastside for a year, the elders and Board of Trustees allowed us the summer in Canada for meetings with Dan Danner leading the singing and traveling with me.

New staff people were added at Columbia Christian College. Bro. T.H. Etheridge became president in June, 1958, and stayed in that office one year. Robert Rowland became dean of academics and in June, 1959, was appointed president and held that office until 1969. A.B. Collett retired from the public schools in Grants Pass, Oregon, and came as a great blessing to the college. He was qualified to teach business and science and had time to serve as our first bursar. It was always good to hear him answer the phone. He would say, "A.B.C. speaking." He served us well for ten years and moved back to Grants Pass. He died in 1987 and willed most of his property to the college. Robert Hooper, from Richland, Washington, came to us and was the head of our history department. He was an able preacher, too. He is now the head of the division of history at David Lipscomb University, Nashville, Tennessee.

Zelma Lawyer was a great blessing to the school and college. She had attended Denton Teacher's College, Harding College, Abilene Christian College, and the University of Southern California. She was skilled in languages and held B.A. and M.A. degrees. We were so glad to have her, especially to teach Latin. Many years after she came to us, Sonny and I were riding in a Jeep on the plains of Kenya when he said, "Daddy, do you know why I am in Kenya?" My reply was, "I suppose it was because of the trip you made for six months with the 'dirty dozen' from Abilene Christian College and Fort Worth Christian College." He retorted, "Never! It was my two years of Latin with Sis. Lawyer. She taught half Latin and half Africa." (Her life had been enriched in Africa as a missionary with her husband, and after he was killed on the field she came home to prepare men and women for the field.)

Time would fail me to name all who did a great job for the college such as: Menzen Dunn, Robert Vance, Robert Stewart, Gerald Long, Phyllis Conrow, Marjorie Hagadorn, Lola Norton, Leona Linscott, Maeve Karr Anderson, and Tonchita Jones Leach.

We were able to keep in touch with the college during the years we were in Australia. During that time, Dr. Rex Johnston became president in 1969 and served until 1974. After him was Dr. J.P. Sanders, 1974 to 1981, followed by Mike Armour, September 1982 to 1986. Dr. Gary Elliott, the husband of our second daughter, Cheryl Ann, became president in 1986 and serves to this present day.

Few honors have come to Sammie and me like the party the college and the Eastside church gave January 26,

1959. (It was after the untimely leaving of Bro. L.D. Webb, serving as acting president for a year, selling the church bonds and raising $50,000 cash for the land and church building and holding the college together until we secured a new president.) The party was a "This is your Life" celebration, and invitations went out to our friends in the church and college. It was a warming and exciting experience. I must state that the ground work for this affair was done by good friends like Curtis and Katherine Danner, Earl and Kitty Butcher, Bill and Joanna Ragsdale and their two daughters, Billye Gay and Johnnie, and Bro. and Sister Earl Smith, Chairman of the Board of Trustees.

Riverside church in Ft. Worth, Texas, supported us the seven years we were in Portland with the college and Eastside church. A letter from that great church was read by Bro. Bob Rowland, the master of ceremonies that night:

Dear Brother Rowland,   January 23, 1959

We realize that Bro. Claude A. Guild's life story would be in complete without a word from his friends in Ft. Worth, Texas, so here we come from Riverside to add our bit—

Claude was enjoying a good work in Corsicana, Texas, when we had himengaged for his first meeting with us in 1948. In this meeting we had wonderful crowds with forty-two responses — twenty-five of these in one service. We decided then that he was the man we needed for our full-time evangelist, so in January, 1949, he began a very fruitful sixyears with us. In this period the church not only grew here and another congregation was established, but we launched out into mission workon such a large scale as we would have formerly believed impossible toaccomplish. Then, one night Claude and Sammie talked to the elders about what was in their hearts — they had decided to go to Portland to work and wanted us to send them; so for the past five years it has been our pleasure to largely support him in this capacity. We have not been disappointed; he has been a "true yoke-fellow."

Words are inadequate to express our deep and abiding love, appreciation and esteem for him and his wonderful wife and and children. A more devoted, consecrated family would indeed be hard to find. We feelthat they have richly deserved all the good things that life can bring. Wehope and pray that God will give them many, many more years of health and strength to continue in His service. We assure you that only the many intervening miles pervent out being there in person tonight.

In Christian love, Elders:
R.H. Banowsky, J.H. Tew, W.C. Sparkman, Glenn M. Holden, Carl Bradshaw and W.E. Stewart

Other nice things were read and said that night and a very large company of friends came from far and wide to share with us. I am very glad that most of my family, including my mother, was able to attend. Bro. Earl Smith had a nice letter for the occasion:

January 26, 1959

Dear Claude,

May I as President of the Board of Trustees of Columbia Christian College express my sincere appreciation for your unfaltering loyalty and efforts

97

on behalf of our school and the church and the splendid way you have rationed your time, energy and work that both the church and school have received a maximum of services and benefit from your work.

God bless you and may your continued interest in our behalf be enlisted.

Yours in Christ,
Earl D. Smith, Chairman

Brother Robert Rowland was a great encouragement at that time, both in the college and in the church. He would do a good job recruiting students, taking care of the college when I had to be gone, an excellent pulpit man in my absence and loyal to the principles of the college and faithful to the ministry. He, too, penned a letter.

January 26, 1959

Dear Bro. Guild:

The faculty and student body of Columbia Christian appreciate all that you have done for our school. We appreciate your zeal, inspiration and unselfish devotion to the cause of Christ. You have melted our hearts many times with your warmth, and you have given us courage when we would otherwise have resorted to panic our forthright approach to your problems and your untiring efforts are deeply appreciated by all. May God give you greater strength, divine wisdom, and a great vision in all your years to come. God grant you will have many years of service and leadership ahead.

We love you,
Brother Robert Rowland, Dean

Time would fail me to mention all the names of people who attended but some are such dear friends: Chester Haven family, Mina Cook, Ellen Massey, Zelma Lawyer, Lola Norton, Cleo and Ed Phillips, Hazel Flanagan, Everett and Mary Gano, Ferd F. Powell, Grant and Mildred Gower, Warren and Amy Higginbotham, H.B. Brattain, Carol and Florence Johnston, Dudley and Blanche Collins, Paul and Thelma Elder, Roy Nash, Hoyle and Elaine Knox, Wendell and Pat Bryant, Curtis and Kathryn Danner, Elmer and Edna Maxwell, Karl Love, Leonard Tester, Joyce Bristol, Tom Bristol, Judie Brisbois, Robert Hooper, Henen Adams, Sis. Nellie Walker, Tant Harmon, T.H. Etheridge, Charles and Dorothy Siler, Kitty and Earl Butcher, Eugene and Edith Altmiller, Johnnie Ragsdale, Bill and Joanna Ragsdale, Sam and Winnie Dusenberry, Anita Jacoby, Chester and Ruby Kennedy, Maeve Karr, Ivan and Aleta Weltzin, Gerald and Betty Long, Dave and Maurice Geiger, Bert and Nona Claspill, Mary Sue Guild, Charles and Orabelle Guild, Ruth McCarroll, Jess and Dorothy Salsma and girls, George Guild, Bob and Phauneal Guild, Cheryl Guild, Charles Carroll, Ella O. Guild, Neaoma and Tony Carroll, Gary Altmiller, Betty Carruthers, Sonny Guild, Charles Godlove, Brian Altmiller, Arthur and Harriett Graham, Thelma Kandel, Curtis and Maud Hardberger, Selma Peck, Hanna Boland, Myra Olson, Luther and Royies Newgent, Bob and Dorothy Preshaw, Sewall and Roberta Magnani, Letha Bunn, Joyce Mortenson, Dude Kennedy, Estel Beaty, Retha Stroud, Juanita Schelot, Sarah Jane Wilson, Carol Rogers, Dorene Simpson, Archie B. Collett and Mary, Marjorey Klobas, Stuart and D'Esta Love, Marguerite Zimmerman, and many, many others including a host of students.

The book they gave me was prefaced with these remarks, "Sometimes when you are associated with a person over a period of years, it is easy to begin to take him for granted. You sometimes forget that even the most understanding person would like an occasional 'pat-on-the-back.'"

"We planned this dinner to demonstrate the old adage that actions speak louder than words. We hope you and Sammie understand you are deeply appreciated by those of us who sign our names before the night is over and by those others who would have been here tonight if possible."

Our evangelistic work continued with meetings at Seminole, Oklahoma, the pulpit occupied by the great and faithful Charles R. Nichols; Midwest City, Oklahoma, with Hugo McCord as the pulpit man; and Odessa, Texas. There were fifty responses in that meeting with eight baptisms — thirty-eight restorations and four who placed membership.

Chapter 8

A CALL TO
FORT WORTH CHRISTIAN COLLEGE

Our work continued at Eastside and the college until May, 1961, when the call came from R.H. Banowsky, elder at Riverside and Board member at Ft. Worth Christian College. He stated bluntly, "We have elected you President of Ft. Worth Christian College." This phone call was totally unexpected and appeared to Sammie and me as a "second touch" from the good city of Ft. Worth, Texas. We visited the college Board and found the following men serving in the leadership of this new college: E.F. Abbott, J.E. Balthrop, R.H. Banowsky, Wade L. Banowsky, W.L. Burlison, Dr. Leo Crowder, Homer Griffin, J.C. Hardy, Roy D. Holland, W.A. Letbetter, Don E. McHam, Roy Mitchener, Jr., Waymond D. Miller, Huey O. Northcutt, J.M. Harvey Norton, Gayle Oler, J. Ed Snelson, George Tipps, L.R. Wilson and Ardis E. Winters.

Thomas B. Warren and Roy Deaver had each served one year as President. The number one problem they were having was finding the funds to operate a Christian college in Ft. Worth. After a review of my responsibilities and a firm commitment from the Board of Trustees, we agreed to accept the new assignment and moved back to Cowtown, June 1, 1961. Our oldest daughter, D'Esta, had married Stuart Love, and they were in Eastland, Texas, with their two sons and our grandsons, Mark and Jon. Stuart was doing graduate work at Abilene Christian College. Cheryl Ann, our second daughter, had finished one year at Abilene Christian

101

College, and it took some doing to get her to transfer to Ft. Worth Christian College after getting roots at Abilene and making friends there. We promised her she could go back to Abilene after one year in Ft. Worth Christian. She would have her A.A. degree. She was willing to come home. When the college had its first football game, Cheryl was dated by a new teacher hired out of Harding College, Gary Elliott. That was the beginning of a courtship that climaxed in August, 1962, with Gary becoming our second son-in-law. Sonny and Mary Sue adjusted well in their new location. We lived in an old parsonage of the Eastridge church until the college finished a nice home for the President two blocks off campus. We then lived on College Hill.

An interesting point about the two colleges is worthy of note. The bursar at Columbia Christian College was Glenn Cash; the bursar at Ft. Worth Christian College was Charlie Money.

Addressing the subject of funds, there were not enough on hand to pay my first two months' wages, and the college was behind on faculty and staff salaries also. We had a fine chorus under the direction of Bro. Dale Welch. We made appointments with various congregations (there were about sixty in the Ft. Worth area), and the chorus sang somewhere every Wednesday and Sunday night. I travelled with them and made appeals. The funds started coming. It was a difficult schedule, because I was preaching at River Oaks and was also ordained as an elder there. It meant that after preaching at home, I would hurry to the congregation where the chorus was performing.

We worked with business and industry for the first time. Most of the banks in Ft. Worth gave to us, especially Haltom City Bank and Richland Hills Bank. We were advised by a former secretary of Don H. Morris that Texas Steel in Ft. Worth was very generous to Abilene Christian College. We visited Mr. George Armstrong, President, and they were not only generous but directed us to others who gave. The various utility companies in Ft. Worth were good to us. With the funds that were coming in, we met the payroll and moved two surplus buildings to the campus, remodelled them for dormitories and bricked them. We also built a very nice gymnasium.

Our goal for finances was to obtain sufficient funds to meet the budget for salaries and current accounts. The Lord was good, and we had a pleasant experience getting the necessary monies. One of the great benefactors of the college was Bro. W.W. Barber. This good man had made a major gift to Abilene Christian College, and, when he saw the student body and the growth we enjoyed, he advised me to come to him on Pershing Drive any month we had a short fall. That great man always met the balance of our payroll each month. We were promised funds through the develop-ment company that was building houses in the area of the college, but those funds never came. But we continued to work hard toward our goal.

Finally, the Abilene Christian College officials made an offer to buy Ft. Worth Christian College and Dallas Christian College. They assumed our indebtedness in the process. It was time for someone to take the leadership through these transitions. Too, the Board offered me an increase in salary, with a world tour after ten years, if I would be just the President of the college and give up preaching. I remembered the pledges I had made to the Lord, and it was impossible to give up the pulpit.

The Lord understood all this, and one Sunday at River Oaks church we had a delegation of elders from the church in Vernon, Texas. They asked for a meeting with me. Bernard Passmore, principal of one of the schools, did the talking at first. We had graduated from Abilene Christian College together, and he had one of his college annuals with him. He read the notation I had made by my name some thirty years earlier, "Bernard, when you get out among them and find it hard going and have difficult times in some church, call on me." Bro. Passmore wanted to know if I was a man of my word. I told him I believed I had been and would be. He continued, "We have a divided congregation, and we need a man like you to put things back together."

Other elders of this fine congregation were T.G. McCord, Cleddie Palmer and Bill Standley. They each used their persuasions and all I could tell them was that we could consider it, but I had a job at Ft. Worth Christian College and at River Oaks. We submitted our resignations at Ft. Worth Christian College and River Oaks and made plans to move to Vernon, Texas. Late December, 1964, my resignation was submitted to the college effective January 28, 1965. In response to my resignation, George Tipps, Chairman of the Board of Trustees, released the following statement: "The Board has been aware of Bro. Guild's desire to give himself more fully to preaching; and, while we know it will be much more difficult to locate a top-notch school administrator than to locate a top-flight preacher, we have accepted Bro. Guild's resignation. The Board is grateful to him for the good he has accomplished here, and commend him to the accomplishment of his first love. His talent and endowments in the pulpit will be used profitably wherever he determines to continue his ministry of the Word."

Serving the Vernon church of Christ, seventy miles west of Wichita Falls and about two hundred miles from Ft. Worth, was a rewarding and endearing experience. The eldership of that congregation had experience and was very well rooted in the Word. They knew how to honor their office with service. Bernard Passmore was one of the finest auditorium Bible teachers I have had the pleasure to hear. Cleddie Palmer was an attorney, and his legal background was helpful many times in our operational procedures. Bill Standlee held an official office with the second largest ranch in Texas, the Waggoner Ranch, with headquarters in Vernon. Bro. T.G. McCord was a principal of schools. These men had great vision for the church.

Division had come to the body of saints in Vernon, and one of the first things we had to do was unite the church. Many things were done, many meetings held and many, many prayers were prayed. Finally, after a year, we recommended that the elders have a meeting with the man over which the division was caused and with his help resolve the differences. I promised to get the man to a meeting with the elders, and the elders would lay before him the major problem, namely, the circumstances under which he left the pulpit as a former minister for the congregation. I visited this man, related how the house was divided, how we were preaching a lot of funerals — twenty-two in one month — and these people were going to eternity with ill feelings, and it ought not to be, and "thou art the man" who can heal the wounds of bitterness. He immediately came to meet with us the next Sunday night. In the meeting with the elders, Cleddie Palmer stated the case, the man went into the auditorium, sat at the communion table, wrote out a statement of apology, and the first draft was accepted. They informed him they would read it the next Sunday morning. He objected because he thought the matter needed his presence, and he would read the statement and cancel his preaching in his local pulpit the next day. He stayed, humbly read his statement of apology and said further, "Elders have enough to do without mending broken hearts and fences caused by division." The whole house was moved to tears. An invitation was extended to all to unite in forgiveness. The elders were the first to gather around the pulpit with this preacher, everyone emptied the pews, we stood as a body before the Lord, prayers were offered by many, forgiveness came, and unity was restored in a great church under a great eldership.

The time had come to go on to bigger and better things. The church was very mission-minded. They immediately took the full support of Bro. Roman G. Cariaga to the Philippines, recommended to them by Bro. Hugo McCord.

They also loved and fully supported Bro. Earl Arnold in Montana. They have continued to carry his support in that state for over forty years.

They planned two meetings a year, along with a great annual lectureship. In 1966 the speakers for the lectureship were Rex Kyker, Chairman of the Speech Department at Abilene Christian College; Joe Barnett, minister of the Broadway Church in Lubbock, Texas; Hugo McCord, Vice President of Oklahoma Christian College; Cleon Lyles, minister of 6th and Isard St., Little Rock, Arkansas; E.R. Harper, Herald of Truth speaker of Abilene, Texas; Judge Jack Pope, Texas Supreme Court Justice, Austin, Texas; and F.W. Mattox, President of Lubbock Christian College.

The church in Vernon (Houston and Peace Streets church) had met in the same building since before the depression. It was a good building, but it had served its purpose. It lacked classrooms for growth, and there were no spaces for work the church needed to do and little office space. The auditorium was hardly large enough for our audiences. It was decided that a new building would be built, and a new location was selected on Wilbarger Street, the main artery through town. The congregation approved the elders' plans, and Bro. Jack Nesbaum of Oklahoma City, Oklahoma, was selected as the architect. A Spanish-type building was erected with ample classrooms, office space, chapel, work rooms, air conditioning and parking space, all of which were not available at the old location. The total cost was over $500,000 for the building alone. A bond drive was issued by the congregation, and I went to work, along with the elders and deacons, and sold the bonds. It was really a joy to me to see this fund raising completed, along with the first Sunday contributions going into the building fund over a long period of time. It was a greater joy to return and see this good church growing, enjoying one of the finest properties in West Texas and even enlarging their mission activities and adding to their eldership.

Sammie and I had talked for several years about returning to foreign mission assignments after the children were grown. Late in 1966 Mack Lyon, former Ft. Worth minister, called on us in Vernon. He and his wife, Golda, and their two children were planning to move to Perth, Australia, for mission work, and he was seeking a companion couple to go with them. He pointed his finger at us. Australia had been in our minds since we were in school with the first missionary to Australia among churches of Christ, Colin Smith. We agreed to go on the condition that Mack Lyon would carry through with his promise of finding our supporting church and sponsoring eldership. We suggested Rosemont in Ft. Worth because they had had a part in our support at Eastside in Portland, Oregon. In a matter of weeks Bro. Lyon phoned and stated that Rosemont would be getting in touch with us. In a few days Charles Hodge, minister at Rosemont, called and inquired, "Did you tell Mack Lyon you would go with him to Australia if he found a supporting church?" I affirmed that conversation, and Charles said, "You and Sammie pack your bags for Australia."

Rosemont church in Ft. Worth, Texas, had been a favorite of ours for a long time. Because we recommended Thomas L. Campbell to them, they volunteered their support to our working fund in Portland for seven years. Now they volunteered to send us to Australia which turned out to be seven years also. Later we will tell you about their supporting us seven years again in Oregon. We agreed to go with the Lyon family.

It was very difficult to leave Vernon, Texas. That church had a super eldership, and they knew how to treat preachers very well. It was the only place I have served where the elders would take time to write me letters of encouragement when I was away in meetings and on other occasions as well. The church furnished a super nice home

107

for its preachers, and the city of Vernon paid the utility bills. The congregation caused us to form warm, lasting friends there — more than any place we had been.

A testing and prayer time had arrived. Would we stay with an ideal preacher's church, love them and they love us and bask in the two things we really wanted to do in Vernon — bring peace to the congregation and get them into a new building? Or would we reach out again in response to the great commission and answer the call to Australia? With a land mass equal to the U.S.A. and thirty congregations, averaging about twenty members per congregation, and twelve preachers on the field, we decided to go to Australia. It meant we would give the Vernon church six months to find another man and get adjusted to the change.

After we gave them six months' notice, the elders invited Eugene Gilmore of Burkburnett, Texas, to succeed us. We had time to visit some congregations to raise our travel funds, $7,000, and find other churches and individuals to assist with our working funds.

Chapter 9

THE CALL TO PERTH, AUSTRALIA

January 10, 1967, we moved into an apartment in Ft. Worth to work with Rosemont three months, raise additional funds for equipment, and get better acquainted with the membership. I also had a heavy schedule of meetings to fulfill. We traveled 16,000 miles and found our travel and working funds and $9,138.50 for equipment and a T.V. program. We also acquired song books, typewriters, Bibles, projectors, films and literature to use in classes in high schools. Funds came from people such as A.M. Burton, Nashville, Tennessee; C.E. Crooks, Goldendale, Washington; Mr. and Mrs. Jerry Cowles, Pasco, Washington; Linda Hurn, Dallas, Texas; Ned Martin, Dallas, Texas; Esta McCombs, Blair, Oklahoma; Mr. and Mrs. Jay Cure, Houston, Texas; Major and Mrs. Ben Acock, Corsicana, Texas; Mr. and Mrs. Ed Clark, Hurst, Texas; Jess and Dorothy Salsma, Elmer Maxwell, Sewall Magnani, A.B. Collett, Jim Wray, Portland, Oregon and many, many others. Churches such as Hillcrest in Arlington; College Church in Abilene, Texas; Saginaw, Springtown, Paradise, Vernon, Grand Prairie, Cross Plains, Rising Star, Spur, South Gate in Los Angeles where Bill Banowsky was preaching, Midwest City with Hugo McCord, Thomas Street in Altus, Oklahoma; Warren, Waurika, Terrel, and Hollis, Oklahoma contributed to our support. And we can never forget the support of our good friends, Lawrence and Altha Richardson.

Finally, we departed from Love Field in Dallas, Texas, April 29, 1967, 11:56 a.m., on American Airlines, flight 27.

The most difficult part of catching this flight was leaving our baby daughter. Although she was just married to Hugh Galyean, and they were in Fort Worth Christian College, she was still our baby. Too, Sonny was in graduate school at Abilene Christian College and preaching regularly at Thalia, Texas, but he was not married yet and liked to come home often. Nevertheless, our children understood our hearts and knew the will of the Lord came first with us, especially with regard to the great commission. We had a great prayer service and family reunion the night before our leaving. The next day we had the prayers and praise of our children, two grandsons, Mark and Jon, and the good brethren from the Rosemont church.

Sammie and I felt nearly criminal. We included on our flight to Australia, a week of resting and vacationing in Hawaii. We had pressed our work so long in so many places we really felt guilty taking off a week in a lovely place, but we did it. This was great for both of us. During the week, the hotel office notified us we had a telegram. Only our children knew where we were, and we thought the worst — something had happened to one of the family. But that was not the case. Dear friends, with whom we had worked many years, Lawrence and Altha Richardson of Ft. Worth, Texas, asked the travel agent for our location and sent the wire. Lawrence and Altha would drive a hundred miles to hear me in a meeting. More than once they heard my sermon on "The New Testament Church." In the sermon I would take a rabbit through a log to show when the church was established. What did the telegram say? "Dear Brother Claude and Sister Sammie, do not forget to take that rabbit through the log when you get to Australia." How wonderful to have great brethren cheering us on as we traveled 10,000 miles from home.

The hour came for us to board a jumbo jet with Qantas (Queensland and Northern Territory Air Service). There would be sixteen hours of water between us and our loved ones, but we would land in the midst of a new field to work.

The plane took us to Fiji Islands, and plans were made to worship with the church there. We landed on the Island of Viti Levu in the city of Nadi. We took a small plane to the Island of Lanva Levu, to the city of Savo. The whole congregation was there to meet us, about sixty people. They walked us to the hotel where we would stay and then to the church building. Great hospitality was shown. Flowers and utensils for eating were presented to us by the mayor of the city. After refreshments, some of the brethren took us for a tour of the city. A special point of interest was a very decorative cemetery of some nineteen graves of American servicemen who gave their lives on the islands during World War II. It was beautifully groomed, with a graceful chain fence around it. The stones were upright and white as snow. I asked permission to read the markings on the stones. I regretted that the names had eroded from the faces of the markers, due to the weather and the softness of the stone.

Sunday came and services were held in a remodeled dwelling. The building was so full there was no standing room. When they came to the Lord's supper, the same elderly black, barefooted man that showed us the cities was in charge of the supper. He remarked about our visiting the cemetery and finding the names washed from the stones. He went on to say, "Bro. and Sis. Guild, we are going to make up for it today. On this table is a memorial that is 1900 years old, and time, weather, fire and all its enemies have never eroded the markings on this memorial feast. It still reads, 'In remembrance of me.'" That was one of the most meaningful Sundays in our lives.

Several missionaries were at the airport in Perth to meet us. They included Rusty Bolton, Ernie Gill, Marvin Phillips, Dale Graham, Mack Lyon and other members of the church. The all-city plan was to have congregations established in four sections of Perth, the great "City of Lights." Mack Lyon and I were to establish the church in the last of the four sections to be evangelized, Riverton. Bro. Lyon was supported by the church in Ada, Oklahoma. Mack left September 5, 1966, and we left May 9, 1967. A hall (formerly a machine shed) was rented, cleaned and fixed up nicely for the new congregation. Bro. Lyon contacted a T.V. station, Channel 9, and was told we could buy fifteen minutes of time for $125.00 a month. I was notified, and my responsibility was to find the support for the program. We approached churches and individuals to buy one Sunday each or contribute $125.00 for the entire month. The response was terrific. The church in Alice, Texas, bought three Sundays; Seagoville two; Cross Plains two; Sis. James Allred, Wichita Falls, Texas, and widow of a former governor of Texas, bought two; Ned and Betty Martin, Dallas, Texas, bought several days; Rosemont church bought time; and churches in Hennessey and Ada, Oklahoma, each bought a day. Members of our family were good to go with the T.V. program. The following bought a day of T.V.: Neaoma and Tony Carroll, Ora Roberts, Earl and Grace Bewley, Ruth McCarroll, and Jess and Dorothy Salsma. Other churches too numerous to mention such as Azle, Thalia, San Jacinto and Amarillo, Texas; and Pueblo, Colorado, bought three Sundays, along with lifetime friends: Lawrence and Altha Richardson, Alvin Neal, both of Ft. Worth; G.R. Landreth, Long Beach, California; Otis Marshall, Springfield, Oregon; and Bud Jones and Dudley Collins, Portland, Oregon.

We bought a home across the street from Mack and Golda Lyon. This was advantageous in that we had one car each, and we could run trips for each other and share their children, which substituted a little for ours we had left at home. All of us had to learn to drive on the wrong side of the road. After a long struggle for me to get my driver's license, Sammie found out you could use your U.S.A. license until

112

you had an accident and then you would have to get an Aussie license. Bless her heart, she never had to get a license during the seven years we were in Australia.

The work grew at Riverton. After the first six months our attendance more than doubled. We grew from twenty-seven to fifty-six. We had weekly articles in the local newspaper, did a lot of letterboxing and taught several cottage classes. As a result, the seed was sown.

One of our greatest finds was Rick Pinczuk of Ukranian extract whose daddy was a Baptist preacher. He had a marvelous mind and was an "A" student. When he got ready for college he wanted to go to America and study for the ministry. We got him a full scholarship at Harding College. He did both his B.A. and M.A. degrees at Harding and went to Canada to get his Ph.D. He accomplished this and married a fine woman. They planned to go behind the iron curtain to preach, but Great Lakes Christian College prevailed upon him to stay there and establish a department of Slavic languages and train others to go to Russia and neighboring countries. He has been a leading church worker for that part of the world.

Immediately we saw the need for a preachers' school and training school for church leaders. Plans were made to make it a city-wide school, and a steering committee was appointed. Bill Moodie was appointed Chairman. Harry Butt was named Vice Chairman, while I was made Corresponding Secretary. (Other committee members were Mack Lyon, Henry Runciman and Edward McGeachy.) We opened with twenty students.

We had Heinrich (Rick) Pinczuk and Ludwig Komorowski in the classes. Ludwig and his mother had come from a labor camp in Russia (they were Polish) where their father died as a slave laborer. Bro. Lyon did a fine job with these families. Ludwig and his mother were Jehovah Witnesses and saw our ad in the paper for correspondence studies and enrolled.

We have long believed it is better to train men at home than send them overseas. They see the wealth, salaries of American preachers and large churches, and few are content to go to their homeland and serve. The success of this school was a great source of joy in our work in Australia and brought maturity and stable leadership to the church.

A National Tour of Australia Planned

Phone calls and letters came to us in Perth about discord in the body among Eastern States churches on the cooperation question. We were being called on by our oldest missionary to Australia, Colin Smith, along with the next oldest, Allan Flaxman. We were not surprised to hear this had happened, because we saw the divisions come to the churches in the Northwest over the same issue. I had written on the issue, and we also had a lectureship at Eastside in Portland with leading men such as E.R. Harper, Dennis Moss, Yater Tant, Maurice Tisdel and others speaking. Bro. Harper published those lectures. Our plans were completed to visit most of the Australian churches and distribute literature and lecture on the issue. Perry Cotham had published some good material, too. We used all the good literature we could command.

Our tour began November 1st, driving to Kalgoorlie. There we took the passenger train and loaded our car on a freight train and carried it across the Nullabor (treeless) Plain 1,200 miles. We picked it up at Port Agusta, and our first meeting was with the church in Canberra. Some fine American families were working there, including Cecil Hutson, Homer Anderson, Fred Bell and George McFarlin. They had worked hard to plant the church in the capitol city. They had seventeen members and were meeting in an auditorium in the shopping mall. It was very nice. We held

114

meetings in many of these cities, including Canberra. Our next stop was in Sydney with Allan Flaxman. He had been in Sydney eighteen years. (He has now been there thirty-eight years.) We had been responsible for his first support when we worked with the Riverside church in Ft. Worth. W.R. Smith, Vice President of Abilene Christian College, brought him to us as a worthy graduating senior, and we accepted his oversight for five years. At the time we arrived he was supported by the church in Enid, Oklahoma. We also held a meeting in Sydney.

Our next stop was in Brisbane, Australia, State of Queensland. We held a meeting with the Holland Park and Wynnum churches. Forest Suddeath, Jr. ministered at Holland Park, along with Lee Newton. They met in a remodeled dwelling. Colin Smith was with the Wynnum church, and they had a nice new building. During those meetings we met with several American missionaries who had gone "anti" like Rollie McDowell. I doubt seriously if we made any headway with any of the men, but we know one thing for sure, we warned the churches and stopped the spread of this difficulty. We also learned on this trip that every other division that had come to American churches had also come to Australia including premillennialism, one-cup, anti-class, anti-located preacher and all the rest.

We travelled 7,400 miles and preached forty times in eighteen of the thirty-three churches in Australia. There were three baptisms in Holland Park and two conversions at Wynnum. It was good to see our old schoolmate, Colin Smith, during this tour. He had been in Australia twenty-seven years without a furlough. All this time he was supported by the College church in Abilene, Texas.

It was good to be back in Perth and by the side of Mack Lyon in the Riverton work. The shop building we had rented was no longer ours. The lease ran out after a year. It was the Lord's will. We found an Anglican building with a nice 30' X 60' auditorium, recreation hall the same size and eight classrooms, offices and restrooms. We had two builders appraise the building, and they figured it would cost us $50,000 to build the same property. The Anglicans were asking $31,000. Bro. Mack Lyon offered them $25,000, and they took the offer. We were back on the job raising funds to pay for it. Brethren in the States were very good to us. Funds came from churches in Oklahoma, Kentucky, Texas, California, Oregon, and from many individuals. It wasn't long until we had half the necessary funds, and we were able to buy the building and move into it.

"Give Diligence
to Come Unto Me Shortly"

March, 1968, came and with the fresh breezes of spring came a sobering request from Colin Smith. He was told by the doctors he had cancer, and they promised him six months to live. His first concern was the church in Wynnum, which he had served ten years, and all the other churches he had helped establish or strengthen: Holland Park, Rockhampton, Emerald, Yepoon, Sellwood, Gympie and Amidale. Since we were classmates at Abilene Christian College, and we had visited earlier in the fall the year before, he called on me to come and replace him. He was certain that without a replacement the anti-cooperation brethren were poised to take the work into their crippling circle.

Sammie and I phoned our elders at Rosemont in Ft. Worth. They asked us to make a tape of our tour and also the request from Colin. We did this, and the word came from the elders to make a move to Brisbane, since there were already seven preachers in Perth and only two in Brisbane with three congregations. April 15, 1968, we made plans to fly to Brisbane. We had, however, the responsibility to sell our home. The Lord was with us and within a month's time the house was sold. We shipped our household effects and

116

car by van and were on our way to our new work.

It became necessary to make a new decision about the building at Riverton. Lots could be bought and a new building could be constructed for the same amount of money, and the brethren made the decision to go with a new plant in the Riverton district. We were pleased that arrangements were made to have a replacement for us at Perth with the coming of Bro. and Sis. Charles L. Brackett, Haskell, Oklahoma. The Southwest church in Ada, Oklahoma, took their oversight.

Chapter 10

THE QUEENSLAND CONQUEST

Why should we leave a good training school, a new work and a beautiful city to go 2,300 miles away to preach? It was the call from Colin Smith in a time of emergency. Colin wrote, "I am deeply grateful to and continuously amazed by my friends, so many of whom have written, expressed concern, petitioned our Heavenly Father and assisted financially when they learned that my health was giving considerable concern. For myself, it has been a tremendous and awe-inspiring experience. I know how it feels to hear a panel of doctors say grimly, 'The outlook is not good.' I know how it feels to look at my family and realize we may not be together long on this earth; to think of my grandchildren and wonder whether I will see them grow up, to move amongst Christians in the church and think that what I say may be the last sermon I may ever preach. I know too that Christ gives a certain air of excitement that is indescribably mingled with this sadness."

"As we give thanks, we realize that Claude Guild will carry on the work after we cried for help. His availability at the time is surely the Lord's doing and assures us that His ways are past finding out."   . . .Colin Smith

Colin Smith was discovered by George A. Klingman. In 1936 he was commissioned by leading brethren in the States to make a world tour and find opportunities to do mission work. In all of Australia, Bro. Klingman reported to the elders of the College church in Abilene, Texas, that he

119

had found a key man for Australia, Colin Smith. He kept himself independent of the digression; he was talented and wanted to get his education. Abilene Christian College offered him a full scholarship. In the fall of 1936 Colin left his wife and son in Hobart, Tasmania, went to Abilene and finished his B.A. degree in three years. He returned to Australia with full support from the College church. After fifteen years in Sydney, he moved to Brisbane to evangelize Queensland. After ten years he was struck down with cancer. He lived eighteen months after our arrival, and they were precious months to me. I consider him the Alexander Campbell of Australia. He labored alone against great odds. He held many religious debates without a moderator; he also answered many calls for long mileage to teach and baptize people all over Australia's eastern shores.

January 10, 1969, the Wynnum church planned a "This is Your Life," party for Colin. It was held at the Shangri La Lounge in Wynnum with Michael Hamilton as chairman. To get Colin there we had a brief celebration for our Bible school teachers. Michael read about his life. He told how Colin's father died when he was eighteen months old, and how he was the first one in his family to finish high school and get a college degree. He related the story of Colin's auto accident at the time he was preparing to return to Australia and how he consequently had to spend seven months in a Houston hospital before returning to his family. He saw his church work of twenty-seven years reviewed. Gifts came from many places, along with letters and telegrams. It was good medicine for both Colin and Sis. Smith.

July 24, 1969, at the age of fifty-nine, Colin Smith fell asleep in Jesus after a three-year battle with cancer. His work will live. He is known among Australian preachers as the "Dean of Aussie preachers." His family asked me to conduct his final crematorium rites on July 26, 1969. Just before his death he called me to his bed and only had brief remarks and a simple request. He expressed no regrets for his service, told me the text to use for his service and requested I write the College church to continue his support to his widow until she got the estate settled.

Before we could get our effects unpacked, word came to us from Manny Company in Ft. Worth, Texas, that my third book was off the presses, <u>Training Men to Preach and Serve</u>. I had taught speech at Columbia Christian College and Ft. Worth Christian College. My notes were completed in the Training School in Perth, and my Rosemont elders and the brethren in Australia encouraged me to put them in permanent form. I completed my manuscript before we left Perth. I am indebted to Winnefred Devlin and Heatherly Payne for typing my final drafts, to Dr. Gary Elliott for proofreading and Linda Hurn, Dallas, Texas, for her splendid art work. This 175 page book dealt with the following subject matter: "Qualifications of a Minister," "The Relevance of Preaching," "Called, Licensed and Ordained," "The Importance of a Good Background," "Applying His First Commission," "His Ability in the Word," "The Importance of Reading and Illustrating," "Your Life is Hid with Christ in God," "The Preacher's Relationship to a Local Church," "Setting an Example," "His Home, Habits, Health, Money and Temptations," "Helpful Hints in His First Services," "Fortunes and Compensations in Preaching."

I am happy to report that the book was used extensively. It was used as a text at Harding College, Four Seas Christian College, McQuarie School of Biblical Studies in Sydney, translated into several languages and used in five preachers' schools in India and most of our preachers' schools in America. We enjoyed two printings of the book, and we still have friends who like to use them in men's training classes in the churches.

The Wynnum Church

The Wynnum congregation was begun by Colin Smith in 1958 with six members from the Associated Church of Christ (Christian Church in America). They first met in an old band hall. The church grew under his leadership until in 1964 they bought land at the corner of Tingal and Chestnut, remodelled an old dwelling, then built their new building the same year. In early 1967 they added a fine classroom building. Wynnum church gave members to many congregations in Australia, and by 1969 they had 100 members — the largest congregation in Australia.

We enjoyed many converts of importance to the work. Trevor Isacs was looking for the Mormon church when he came to our place of worship. It was too late to direct him so he stayed with us. That was in July. He continued to stay and by October 20th he obeyed the gospel and became a force for good.

Rosalie Coward was a story-book girl. Her story was so typical of the young people at the Wynnum church. Rosalie's father died when she was just a child, and he left the mother with five children. Rosie didn't get to finish junior high school because she had to go into the fields and work to take care of the others. After she saw her baby sister married to a fine man from Rockhampton, Qld., she wanted to do something with her life.

After picking up my mail one day, Rosalie came up to our home and asked me what she could do to be worth something to the world. In my handful of mail was a bulletin I had gotten for years, "The Boles Home News." I said, "Rosie, prepare to be a nurse. One day we will have an orphanage in Queensland, and we will need your services. Look, Rosie, I have an orphanage bulletin from the U.S.A. and I know the director, Gayle Oler, and I baptized their director of development, Thomas Seay. You could even work for them until we get an orphanage." She related to me that she had always wanted to be a nurse, but she could not go to nurses' training without a junior leaving certificate. "How can I at twenty years old go to junior high school and finish," she said. I told her I was fifty-three and teaching scripture classes in junior high schools, and she could go with me and it would be fine. To this she agreed, got her uniform, enrolled and sat in classes with little fourteen-year-olds. She graduated with four A's, one B and one C. February 10, 1969, she was accepted in the Royal Princess Alexander Hospital for nursing. She was a one young person. After three years in Brisbane, she went to Sydney to specialize. We lost touch with Rosie after that.

January, 1973, we got a letter from Rosie, and she was, of all places, assigned to a nursing position in Scott-White Hospital in Temple, Texas. She served there two years and when we returned to the States and visited Linda Hurn in Dallas, Texas, there was Rosie. She lived sixty miles north of Dallas, serving as a nurse in Boles Home, Quinlan, Texas. God bless this girl, but you must hear the rest of the story. She opened her purse, took out a worn and ragged bulletin. It was the one from Boles Home I gave her in 1968. She went on to tell us that she determined that one day she would nurse in that home in Quinlan, Texas, and she had arrived. You would think that was the end of the story, but she met a fine man, Pat Odell, who had finished at Preston Road School of Biblical Studies. They married and went back to Queensland. They have served the churches well for several years and are still there and have four fine children.

Our Wynnum work was enhanced with the services of several ladies. Dr. Phillip Barker was a chiropodist and wanted to do service for Christ by offering people foot care that couldn't afford it. (The climate was about like Jacksonville, Florida, lots of people went barefoot, and there were many more foot problems than we have here.) She asked permission to install a chair and cabinets in a classroom to treat the people, and Sis. Colin Smith assisted her. Many came, all were given literature, and some came to Christ through these fine ladies who "labored with me in the gospel." I could have said, "They helped me as we shod them with the gospel of the preparation of peace."

There were so many it is hard to point to just a few, but, I must tell you about Arthur and Jan Bowell. Michael and Sandra Hamilton made a home for for them eight weeks while they got settled from England. Jan soon obeyed the gospel but Arthur was not church-minded. When Jan was ill, I can remember Arthur bringing the children, letting them off by the church door and running back to his car as though something might fall on him or bite him. He got to know us through trips for the Sunday school children, and he obeyed the gospel. Today he is one of the leaders in the church at Wynnum. Jan's mother, Doris Mumbray, came from England. Jan bragged about their "Yank" preacher at the church, but Doris remembered the war years in England and declared, "I have never met a yank I ever liked." But, she came and I just couldn't remember her name, Mumbray. Hence, at the door I said to her, "Sweetie pie, I want you to come back." She went home thrilled with the "yank" she had met and said, "Guess what he called me? He called me Sweetie pie."

Six months passed, and we saw Doris at the veggie store, and she had an unusual request. She wanted to be baptized. But having not seen an immersion, she wanted to go to the building and have a rehearsal. I took her up there, took her in the water and actually put her under. She was surprised that I didn't put her in face forward. The next Sunday I immersed her, and before she left the baptistry she said, "See there, that wasn't too difficult, in fact there wasn't anything bad about it." We always gave them baptismal certificates in the "Now that I'm a Christian" booklets. Sandra filled it out and put in Doris' full name. The next Sunday she brought it back to me and said, "Preacher, you made a mistake on my certificate." I read it over, and it looked perfect to me, but she went on to say, "I want the 'Doris' part removed, and I want you to write in there, 'Sweetie Pie.'" Although I have known her twenty years now, she is still "Sweetie Pie" in all our letters.

Scripture Classes in Public Schools

Bro. Colin Smith had two classes going in Wynnum in the two high schools. I taught them after he was unable to go to class. I thought about the United States. Longer than I can remember they have expelled the Bible from our public schools and now they have expelled prayer. These people have done neither. We began expanding these classes. We had them in several suburbs, but in Holland Park and Wynnum especially. They requested through the Headmaster a curriculum schedule of the courses we would offer; they would be examined and approved. We never had one turned down. They would assign us a room, print our schedule and announce the classes at the opening of school.

At our best we had thirty-eight classes going in nineteen schools. I had to go home in January, 1970, and arrange for more teachers. I found them. Randy and Marlene Baker were at Ft. Worth Christian Schools. Randy heard a missionary speak from Australia at Harding chapel. He was touched and carved on a piece of bark from a tree the word "Australia." When this ol' Alabama boy was out of money and didn't know how he could continue college, he would look at that bark and hold on because he believed one day he would go to Australia. He worked for the Brentwood church, and they underwrote his support. Marlene taught in the public schools, so they were a perfect couple for the job. We recruited Hugh and Mary Sue Galyean. (Mary Sue is our

125

youngest daughter.) Hugh was the minister at Shreveport, Louisiana, and they underwrote his support.

We were able to get a lovely lady, retired Dean of Women at Lubbock Christian College, Audean Baldwin. She was very qualified to teach Bible and worked out to be a perfect hostess to visitors to the congregation. She had a good friend, Anna B. Odell, the widow of a leading lawyer in Lubbock. She was a typical West Texas lady with a lot of grace and class for the saints in Brisbane. An ideal choice was Ruby Ellis of Yakima, Washington. We had mailed our bulletins to Sis. Montgomery for years. We appealed in one issue for a church secretary for the Holland Park church. Ruby had just retired as head of the Land Division of Indian Affairs in the state of Washington and wanted to be a missionary. Sis. Montgomery gave her the bulletin and in two weeks time she was packed and on her way to us.

Clyde Baggett, Los Angeles barber from a loyal church family, came to establish his own business and be self-supporting. Twenty years have passed, and Clyde is still working in Australia. Ed and Janice Glover, Sumter, South Carolina, came well recommended to us by W.A. Bradfield of Freed Hardeman College. Last but not least was Stephen Clayton of Vernon, Texas. He came for a summer to teach and preach for us. He was effective — having baptized four people — and was a great hit with our young people in Australia.

The talent in the Wynnum church was unlimited. They could make materials for their own Bible schools, vacation Bible schools, parties and you name it. After several more years with the Queensland work, Wynnum church gave us a farewell party as we sailed on the Himalaya for home. They composed a song to the tune of "Jimmy Brown" and sang it to us. It is worth printing:

There's a little church, down by the bayside,
Where people worship every week

And there on a Sunday morning
Claude and Sammie came to speak.
All the local folks were singing
Every parent, every child,
And the thoughts that they sent winging
Were for Claude and Sammie Guild.

Then the Wynnum congregation
Prayed for guidance from above
Save our ears from strangulation
May we learn Claude's voice to love.

There's a little church, down by the bayside
Where Claude and Sammie preached for years
Till the local population
Scarcely could believe its ears.
All the local drivers knew him
In his mighty Morris car,
Oftentimes they nearly slew him
Loudly cursing from afar.

Then the Wynnum congregation
Prayed for guidance from on high
Lead us not into temptation
Save us from this provocation
Help us teach him how to fly.

There's a little church, down by the bayside
Where many members had strange looks
For they'd come to hear some preaching
But hear Claude Guild sell his books
All the local members wondered
Why he went to India
But they found that they had blundered
When they had to pay his fare.

127

Then the Wynnum congregation
Prayed for guidance from on high
Lead us not into temptation
Please protect the Indian nation
Against Claude Guild's watchful eye.

From the little church, down by the bayside
To many places they did roam
And then abroad the Himalaya
Claude and Sammie Guild went home.
It is pleasant to remember
All the happy meetings shared
That for every single member
We know Claude and Sammie cared.

Then the Wynnum congregation
Prayed for guidance from above,
Lead us not into temptation
As we show our acclamation
And we send them all our love.

Forrest Suddeath, Holland Park, had been a school
teacher prior to his preaching for them. Lee Newton,
Naturopathic physician, also helped with the preaching.
They called on Sammie and me to help them work out a plan
for a new building and find ways and means for a T.V.
program in Brisbane.

The Holland Park Focus Begins

January 10, 1969, a building committee was established, and we were invited to their first meeting. The church
owned a remodeled dwelling with a tin roof for a meeting
place. They had bought some lots, but they had turned
commercial and had to be sold. The church had fifty-three

members and some were professional and good business people. They included Bill and Ed Selbourne who owned a steel fabrication company and Ross Leggatt who was State Director of Construction for Ampol Oil Company of Queensland.

The banks would not give them a loan until they raised one half the funds for the building. If they could sell the lots and dwelling and find $5,000 they could get a loan and get on with the building. My job was to help them find the $5,000. This congregation held real promise. They also made overtures to us to come with them as their pulpit minister.

Sammie and I did a lot of heart searching and praying. We had $5,000 in savings in America to help us buy a home when we returned home. (We went to Australia to stay two years and already we had passed that time frame. We finally prayed to the Lord that we would give Holland Park our $5,000 toward their building funds and make an appeal to replace them in the Queensland Progress Report. If the funds came back we would know the Lord wanted us to buy a home in Queensland and stay with Holland Park.) We furnished the funds, made the appeal and the funds came back. We stayed in Queensland, bought a home and moved to this working, ambitious congregation. (Wynnum had Keith More finishing at Sunset School of Preaching in Lubbock, Texas, and Hugh Galyean, our son-in-law, was coming from Shreveport, Louisiana, and both of these men would work with the Wynnum congregation.)

Regular visitors to Brisbane were Mr. George Kimbell and his wife, Ruth, of Wichita Falls, Texas. Mr. George was not a member of the church, but Ruth was a very faithful member. Mr. George asked us on one visit (they owned land and feed lots in the outback of Queensland and came to tend their properties) about our building plans. It was hard for them and others to hear when it rained or hailed in the tin-roofed dwelling. Ross Leggatt, draftsman, drew plans for a new brick building: full basement for classes, auditorium seating 250 people, offices, nursery and restrooms. The Selbourne brothers would raise the superstructure in steel. The property sold and in February, 1969, the groundbreaking took place, and we were on our way. The Kimbells were generous to us, and, since his death, Sis. Ruth Kimbell has helped in our work around the world, even now in Portland with Columbia Christian College.

Since we mentioned Mr. and Mrs. Kimbell, we should also mention others who played a large financial part in our work on a regular basis: Mr. and Mrs. L.W. Richardson of Ft. Worth, Texas; the College St. church of Christ of Junction, Texas; South Gate church of Christ in South Gate, California; Church of Christ, Alice, Texas; 10th and Broad St. church of Christ in Wichita Falls, Texas; Burkett, Texas, church of Christ; Mrs. Jimmie Allred of Wichita Falls, Texas; Mr. and Mrs. Ned Martin of Dallas, Texas; Belmont church of Christ in Pueblo, Colorado; Mr. G.R. Hill of Seagoville, Texas; Cowan Hutton of Rising Star, Texas; Linda Hurn of Dallas, Texas; Bro. Edward E. Davis of Dallas, Texas; Mr. and Mrs. Homer Steadman of Ft. Worth, Texas, Mrs. Roy Arrowood of Cross Plains, Texas; Dr. John Paul Gipson of Abilene, Texas; Park Row church of Christ, Arlington, Texas; Pauline Cowles of Pasco, Washington; Mozelle Richardson of Cross Plains, Texas; J.F. Crisman of Chattanooga, Tennessee; Wynnewood Hills church of Christ of Dallas, Texas; Bell Trust, Dallas, Texas; Mr. and Mrs. A.B. Tenny of Okemah, Oklahoma; Mrs. G.R. Landreth of Long Beach, California; Miss Helen Powell, Hurst, Texas; Myra Writer of Edmonds, Washington; Bettye B. Still of Seattle, Washington; Mr. and Mrs. Charlie Lewis, Ft. Worth, Texas; Mr. and Mrs. Charles Andrews of Ft. Worth, Texas; Mr. and Mrs. Russell Cope, Ft. Worth, Texas; and A.B. Collett of Grants Pass, Oregon. The help from these named above, carried our support, monies for buildings, T.V., radio and supplies for public school classes and transportation to India, Singapore and related countries.

We planned a number of gospel meetings for Wynnum and Holland Park. We have always believed there is no substitute for sowing the seed. Some of the men who came for meetings were Hugo McCord, Thomas L. Campbell, Bob Wilkerson, Gary Elliott, Jerry Jones, Guss Eoff, Joe Cannon and Roy Roper.

Camp Gidawarra

The churches in Queensland had never had a camp experience. Sammie and I traveled extensively to find a place to rent and arrange a summer camp for children. We finally found Camp Guidawarra on Mt. Tamborine. We set a date to rent it and sent out invitations to young people. The enrollment was very small the first year. It amused us to see the parents come and visit, look around, try the food, and see what was being done and taught. These visits sold them for the next year. The camp has been in operation twenty years now, and they are having men, women and young people's retreats and camps and if Sammie and I didn't go to Australia for any other reason, it was worth it all to have established the camp on Mt. Tamborine. There have been hundreds of baptisms as a result of the camp.

There was one girl I recall very well that worked in Brisbane and drove out to camp every night. She was Elaine Leggatt, formerly Elaine Newton, adopted in New York by the Lee Newton family after they met her at Camp Shilo in the Northeast. She had such fond memories of Camp Shilo she had to come to camp and still does.

Super People at Holland Park

Bill and Audrey Selbourne had built a friendship with Dave Hartley over a period of ten years. (Bill and Dave were big men, and I mean BIG.) I have related earlier how Bill and his brother Ed were in the steel fabrication business. I had been to their plant when one of them would get a catch in his lower back. The other one would put a chain around the other's ankles, raise him twenty feet high with a crane and jerk the cable from the crane a few times. They would swear it was good therapy for back trouble. Bill and Audrey were able Bible students and taught Dave, and he was baptized into Christ.

They sat together in church, Bill on one side of Dave and Audrey on the other. When I referred to passages of scripture during sermons, the Selbournes had no problem turning to the text. Dave was completely lost. He didn't know Old Testament texts from New Testament. After the third Sunday, Dave came to me as I was leaving the pulpit and said, "I would like to make a suggestion if I may." We welcomed his suggestion and he continued, "Instead of giving the book, chapter and verse like you have been doing, wouldn't it be easier for all of us if you would just give the page number?" Well, there may have been fifty different Bibles in the house. I know how Dave must have felt a year later when he found out how infant-like his request must have been.

Another great conversion was Rahila Deen, a secretary in one of the high schools where we had scripture classes (McGregor High School). She was a Pakistani Muslim, saw us on Channel 9 T.V. and asked to have a study. The study, including the teaching of Stephen Clayton of Vernon, Texas, did it. After she was converted, we reached her brothers, Sayd and Joe. Later we reached her sister, Kim, and her husband, Rodney Smith. Her mother came to church very faithfully, loved the church people, and the church loved her. We left Holland Park in February, 1973, without seeing her converted. Randy Baker, my associate, stayed on with the ministry there. In less than a year we had a cablegram from Randy and it read, "She is no longer mother Deen; she is Sister Deen." The great mother of all those Deens had obeyed her Lord. She is even now a very faithful Christian.

Holland Park was blessed with a number of solid citizens among the mature families. Bill Selbourne would match any auditorium class teacher in the States. He built a fine library and really had a thirst for truth. His brother Ed is able to preach and is an excellent song leader. Their wives, Audrey and Vi respectively, are just as talented. These families donated land in the Tana Mera district of Brisbane to have another congregation. Three things have to take place to make a migration of brethren to a new location without a split: let the home church give their blessing to the exodus, have the home church pick the talent to lead the new work and see that the necessary funds come from the parent church. Over a period of five years Holland Park worked to plant the gospel in Tana Mera. The new congregation is healthy, and Holland Park continues to excel.

Ian and Doris Holland are talented and a great host and hostess for the church. Their home was also a place for great Bible studies, and he served as treasurer of the church for years. They helped with "Meals on Wheels" and served as taxi for many of the Bible teachers that came from America like Sisters Ellis, Baldwin and Odell. They are the salt of the earth.

Ruth Leggatt and Isabel Massey were two ladies that drove perhaps twenty miles every Sunday to church, and they made it even on Wednesday nights. Ruth's husband cooked in the outback in sheep and cattle camps, and Isabel had a frock shop. When special drives were made to find funds to do things that had to be done, we could count on

Ruth and Isabel. There were times and there will always be times when preachers need a word of encouragement, a press of the hand, a warm and friendly smile of endorsement, and these ladies helped us carry on. It was Ruth's son, Ross, that drew up the plans for our nice building at Holland Park. He and his mother were Methodists. In Ruth's zeal for souls, she brought Isabel, a member of the Associated church, and Sister Joyce Kruger, Anglican. Her daughter-in-law, Elaine, was a fine Bible teacher, too.

Another great convert was Leo Livingood. A man with a name like that should have been a Christian all his life. He was originally from Hamlin, Kansas, and a distant relative of past President Dwight D. Eisenhower. He was a radio operator on a shrimp boat. He read his Bible, listened to his radio and when in harbor got our T.V. program. He wrote in response to our radio program and soon believed he needed to be immersed. His next shore leave, he saw a church in the distance and walked there on a Sunday morning. The Anglican priest treated him royally, but when Leo asked to be immersed, he was put off because the priest said, "I have never immersed anyone and I would like a little time to think about it." Leo lived in fear during his next trip at sea. Two weeks passed, and he hurried to the same church and renewed his request. The priest said he had thought about it but having never immersed anyone he was afraid he would make a mess of it and advised him to find another church.

Leo looked us up and was waiting at the church steps as we came for Bible school. He made his request, and we gladly offered to immerse him. But, he said, "I live on the water, and I prefer running water to a baptistry." I related to him I knew the perfect place on the Pacific Golf Course. I told him about the many balls I had shot into the creek, and it would be a joy to get back at that stream by using it for baptism. He took lunch with us and used some of my clothes. After his baptism — Sammie witnessing it — he asked to lead in prayer prior to leaving the stream. He prayed, "Lord, I am a little child. Help me to grow. Lord, I am a little lamb, help me to hear the voice of the Great Shepherd and grow up to be a good sheep." Amen. How exciting to see a newborn pray that simple but serious prayer.

You won't believe the things that happened with regard to this next family. We put an ad in the local paper indicating that we were looking for twenty children to take to camp. After placing the ad, fifty children applied. We interviewed them and picked twenty. In that number were Janet and John Pillinger. They were good campers, came to our Sunday school, and the mother, Betty Pillinger, asked for a study. Randy Baker studied with her, and she was baptized. John was soon a Christian and shortly thereafter his oldest sister, Marjorie, was baptized. It didn't take long to reach Marjorie's fiance, Fred Faulkner. Janet also came to Christ and last, but not least, Al Pillinger, the daddy of the bunch, obeyed the gospel. He was baptized the same night that Roslyn Barker, office mate to Rahila Deen, was baptized. All spoke affectionately of her as "his twin sister in Christ." Soon after his baptism, he prepared a barbeque for several families, including Randy and Marlene, who were champions at conducting cottage classes, especially with this large and great family. When the meal was prepared, Mr. Al said, "Well, I know this may shock some of you, but I plan to make a test run at praying." He did a good job, and everyone was filled with joy and encouraged him. As the years have passed, he has filled the pulpit for a number of congregations in the area.

At one time we carried some children to the meetings, and they were from a Nunn family. Likewise, we had two families in the church, faithful members, named Cardinal. John Cardinal retired from a sizable department chain, Myers Stores. It was confusing in our reports back home when we would tell them we had Cardinals and Nunns in the church in Australia.

135

Our love for and memory of Ruby K. Ellis never ceases. You may wonder why we published the "Queensland Progress Report," "The Northwest Report" and now "The Challenge of Africa." There are many good reasons, which include keeping the people informed at home and attracting personnel for our work. This is where Ruby fits in. We also used these bulletins to give brethren back home an opportunity to have a part in the work financially. Ruby's neighbor, Sister Montgomery of Yakima, Washington, received the bulletin, and I have already related how she gave the bulletin to Ruby. That was the beginning of Ruby's great work in Australia.

You need to know that thirty years earlier Ruby's husband was killed on the railroad, and she was left on her sick bed with two small children. A good man in the church told her if she would get out of the bed, get strength enough to sit in a wheelchair, he would give her a filing job in the Indian Bureau. Ruby had serious arthritis. Her diet was changed and other good things happened to her health, and now she is able to walk. She developed professionally and eventually headed the Land Management Department. Although her hands and feet were knotted when she came to us, she could type like the wind and had an angelic disposition toward the work, people and souls. She wanted to teach scripture classes in the schools, and we let her do that.

When we came to America for our next assignment by the elders of the Rosemont church, Ruby came with us and served wonderfully in Tigard, Oregon. Finally the time came, because of the dampness in Oregon, when she had to go to Montana and live with her daughter. She became acquainted with Columbia Christian College while in Portland and in the latter ten years of her life contributed greatly to the school. She also helped direct the Dick Wagner family to Portland as teachers. God bless the memory of this great soldier of the cross.

Time would fail me if I mentioned all the people who helped with the work in Holland Park. Gordon Blackmore, a leader with the deaf group that worked with us, really believed he was saved to save others. He was successful in the work and was responsible for converting Sister J. Turner. Charlie and Dulcie Annand were good church people. Charlie was a building contractor, but he was always willing to take his children to youth activities, and Dulcie was by his side. They came to prayer meetings when others stayed home. He learned to preside and teach. He hauled a lot of people to church, includeding Mary Dimitriou. It resulted in Mary's conversion and those of her two daughters, Patricia and Marina. Mary in turn became a great worker, especially in our "Meals on Wheels" program. She cooked at camp along with Mary Edwards. Yanks would snicker at the closing dish at camp. They combined their scraps in a soup-like dish. It would include bacon, scrambled eggs, cabbage and other veggies. They called it "Bubble and Squeak." What an Aussie dish to close camp meetings.

Among the American teachers of the scriptures was a delightful lady, retired Dean of Women from Lubbock Christian College, Audean Baldwin. Her son, an automobile dealer in Colorado, gave her a new Holden car. (The only car made in Australia.) She had difficulty driving it but gave it to the missionaries to use. She called it her "Gospel chariot." She lived three houses from the church building. When people were converted, Audean would entertain them in her home with beautiful refreshments. She helped make converts like Phyllis Manser. She taught eight classes a week in religious instruction. She had two classes in her home for girls, one in sewing and another in Bible. She cared for the nursery during worship. This dear lady also graded correspondence courses. She was a person who never missed an opportunity to teach and serve people.

137

God bless the work of Randy and Marlene Baker in Aussieland. They were cool under fire, he was and is a great preacher, and they accepted Aussie ways as well as any missionary. They even lived in a home with a "dumpty-do" (outdoor toilet). Randy and Marlene were supported and overseen by the Brentwood church in Ft. Worth, Texas. This is a good overseeing church. Bob Bankes is the minister. It was a great delight to see one of his elders, Pete and Hazel Fry, come to see the work. As our work with American involvement slowed to make them self-supporting, it was my serious decision to leave the work at the last with Randy and Marlene. He was a good soldier and today ministers in Florence, Alabama.

I either should write another book or take a few minutes to tell of the Hollanders, the Tom Bunt family, in the congregation. Tom provided great leadership and went on to New Guinea as a missionary. I should tell of the Chinese brethren, Roy and Bill Leong. Bill did our lawn for years. He would not take money in an open hand but would only receive it in an envelope. He would weed the cracks in the sidewalks, wash the garage inside if left open, wash the car if left out and would never eat lunch with us unless he could do the dishes. He and his brother were refreshing and delightful. There were so many nationalities represented in the congregation that when the international President of Kiwanis visited our services, Mr. Bob Rogers, he was amazed at the mixture of people. The next day at the national convention in So. Australia he said, "I went to church at Holland Park church of Christ Sunday in Brisbane, Queeensland, and I saw so many nationalities I thought I was in the United Nations. Mr. Rogers was from Kansas and not used to mixed races of people. There was also Jan and Susan Rumble who found the church through our vacation Bible school. They went to work immediately. Their first assignment was to fix the communion service. I could name the Bob Tape family, Doug Symonds family, Hilton Murphys,

Derrick and Christine Roberts from So. Africa, Merida Smith and her husband who heard the truth on T.V., took the correspondence course and obeyed the gospel. Jo Ann Homann, former Roman Catholic, was brought by Allan Hibberd who converted and later married her. Ann Dunn, eighty-seven years young, found Christ through our T.V. program, also. Joan and Noel Andrews came to us from New Zealand. He used his printing talent for the church. Raoul and Robyn Sjolanders, Lutherans, also came to one of our gospel meetings. She obeyed the gospel first but thought he would not come to the meeting on Friday night because that was his night to go to the races. But he came and that was his night of decision to obey the gospel.

Sammie taught a girls' class which was very successful. She taught the gospel to them, which resulted in several conversions, including an Aboriginal girl. They learned the proper length to wear their dresses, how to be homemakers, and how to be Christian in their dating. It was a very large class.

It was a common practice among members to write us a letter about their conversions, and we have a scrapbook filled with them. I wish I could give all of them in this volume, but let me give three from girls who were students in Sammie's class. Susan Rumball wrote, "Jan, Kym, Peter and I went to the Vacation Bible School in 1970. The lessons and teachers were great. Our parents came for the presentation of certificates. Our family was greeted by the people who were later to become my brothers and sisters in Christ. The smiles, handshakes were warm and friendly, the wish to see us at church again was sincere. Jan and I started coming. Bro. Norm and Sis. Faith Cardinal came to our home and talked to our parents about being baptized. He explained fully about what it was to be a Christian. My parents did not respond but Jan and I knew this is what we must do. The next Sunday Faith led us up the aisle during the invitation song. We took turns confessing before the

139

congregation that Jesus Christ is the Son of God. Jan was baptized first; then it was my turn. Bro. Cardinal lowered me into the water, and I was baptized and knew I was saved. In that short space of time of rejoicing, I gained brothers and sisters all over the world, my sins were washed away and I was in Christ."

Diane wrote, "I was raised a Methodist and in my teens my religion didn't mean much to me, but when I began teaching Sunday school, I liked that. I met a young man, Ian Coker, member of the church of Christ. He pointed up a lot of truths to me like using only the Bible as religious authority. I attended a few services with him, was encouraged to take a correspondence course, and when I closed the last lesson I knew I had been missing a lot. It was either take the Bible completely or ignore it all. There was no compromise. June 6, 1971, was Sunday and I made my decision to obey the gospel. During services I was so excited I felt like crying. At the close I was baptized and was so happy I could have hugged everyone, because I had become a sister of the members of Christ's church."

I am glad to tell you that Ian and Diane fell in love, and we had the pleasure of uniting them in marriage. We carried them to Sydney, and he enrolled in McQuarie School of Biblical Studies, graduated and took the church in Toowoomba. He has faithfully served as an evangelist there for fifteen years. They have four children and are terrific workers.

Janet Pillinger wrote, "As a result of an ad in the newspaper, I was selected by the church of Christ to be a camper on Mt. Tamborine. I came home with a resolve to be a better person. I attended their Vacation Bible School. This school gave me a better understanding of the Bible. I began attending church worship, and it was there that I learned how to become a Christian. I met a wonderful person, Audean Baldwin, who became helpful to me in many ways. She started me doing a Bible correspondence

140

course which unfolded God's way for people just like me. My mother was now baptized and Randy Baker was having classes in our home. I was rather shocked when my sister, Marjorie, made the good confession. All of these guided me into a need to obey the gospel. After infinite sermons by my mother and much thought on my part, I decided that I must be baptized before it was too late. I am so glad I was led to Christ by these wonderful people."

The teaching process continued for these girls with Sammie's class. They were quick to learn, and they were evangelistic in their responses to other people. Many of them were taking Bible in scripture classes in their school. We used a method of teaching where they marked their Bibles according to subject matter in colors. The subject was identified in the front of their Bibles and carried to the first passage, then that one would carry to the next passage. The greatest blessing would come when parents would phone and inquire, "May we mark our Bibles too? The children are enjoying this so much and it is so simple, we want to go along with them in the study." We would reach their children and then go to their homes and the parents were ready for conversion. Wouldn't it be good if we could do this in the public schools in America?

Chapter 11

THE ELDERS CALL FOR A HOME ASSIGNMENT

After nearly seven years with the Australian involvement, the Rosemont elders made a trip through Utah, Idaho, British Columbia, Washington and Oregon looking for a field of at least 50,000 in population, steady employment, higher than average income people and no church of Christ. They met Walter Burkett, full-time elder at Eastside, and he assured them he knew the place they were looking for. He drove them to the Tigard\Lake Oswego\Tualatin area southwest of Portland and west of the Willamette River. There were almost 160,000 people west of the Willamette River and only one congregation, namely, the Beaverton church of Christ. In the language of Brigham Young, Walter said, "This is the place."

The elders phoned us in Australia and told us what they had in mind. We would come home, take a week for vacation and another week to turn our working-fund people in the direction of the Northwest and begin a church in Tigard, Oregon. The most I could remember about Tigard was prune orchards and berry fields, but great expansion had gone in that direction and it was difficult to believe what we saw. The Washington Mall, second in size only to Lloyd's Center Mall, acres of flats and thousands of homes going up.

It was difficult to have the good-byes at Brisbane, but they had to come. We advised the Americans first and planned a rotation of disengagement beginning with Bro. and Sis. Ed Glover, Sammie and I would be next to the last to leave, with Randy and Marlene Baker the last. A lot of work had gone into training local people to tend the scripture classes. Our home sold easily, and we booked passage on a ship to return. Twenty-one days on the water, with forty cubic feet of space for each of us, for our household things and my library and equipment, came to the same price as two airline tickets. Let me recommend this to every missionary. It is rest for your body, mind and spirit. We were ready for a new work. A prospectus was prepared in advance for this new work, and it is a good working model for any church-missionary relationship in a new field. Read it with care.

The Prospectus

Paul and Barnabas returned to Antioch in Syria to report "what great things God had done and how a great door of faith had been opened to the Gentiles." We felt the need to return and report to the churches that had sent us into the field. Knowing that Holland Park was reaching a mature state where we could wind down the American involvement, we requested the Rosemont elders to make ready our plans to return for the above trip, and it was also thought best we should locate closer to home base for awhile. Glenn Albricht, Cline Paden, Jack Exum, Wayman Miller and others have been most gracious in making a review of our all-over relationship. With this Prospectus it will improve our total missionary effort and in the process, strengthen the "ties that bind."
Very general criteria were laid out by them as much as six months ago and great efforts on their part have been exhausted to make this transition. In the meantime they directed me to put forth my best at Holland Park and this we

have tried to do. Too, we have added a few thoughts to their criteria suggestions:

1.   The new assignment "should be located in a metropolitan area with a population of a minimum of 50,000 people so more can be reached more quickly and the gospel radiate out. This was true of Paul in his missionary journeys. Further, we feel that this area should have a vigorous, stable economy with a solid economic base and a strong growth potential. This is opposed to an economically depressed area which would stand generally to lose rather than gain population during the next few years," the elders stated.

The above suggestion is very good. We had asked that when the time came for reassignment, it could be in the Northwest, U.S.A. We had given fifteen years to the area, know the people and the potential and since there are so many fields, this would be ideal for us. The elders were thoughtful to consider this.

2.   The elders stated, "This area should be in a mission field — that is, no church in the general area, or the church in the general area is very weak and no church at all in the immediate area. We want to locate in an area where there is a crying need for the gospel and at the same time a favorable economic climate otherwise. We anticipate no real serious problem in 'selling Rosemont' on this move if we can point out the areas where there is a locally identifiable need and an opportunity (in the form of Claude Guild) to fill this need with the gospel."

To illustrate how the eldership worked, not in word only but also in deed, they planned a 6,000 mile survey trip with an elder making the survey. He traveled objectively, thoughtfully and talked with people in Utah, Idaho, Oregon, Washington, and Montana. He held many conferences with leaders of the churches in the general Northwest and reported back that they had found an ideal location of 160,000 people with no church in the Tigard\Oswego area and five churches in the general area of 600,000 people in metropolitan Portland, Oregon. The elders phoned and asked if we would accept an assignment to that location. We told them we had prayed that whatever the elders found would be the answer to our prayers and that we would be willing to go.

Enough cannot be said about the hours of meetings, phone calls, letter writing and miles traveled by the elders to locate the right place, under the right circumstances for this work. They have word that there are at least twenty two members living in the area that attend at Westside (Beaverton) but the Westside elders are happy to cooperate with a new work in this very busy, growing area of Portland even to the point of giving up these families to the new work.

3. The Rosemont elders have stated further, "We want to set a goal in making such a work self-supporting in a reasonable time and feel that all planning should be toward this end. This will require a great amount of time spent in this local area and a minimum of time away from it. It also will require a great amount of personal teaching in homes, person-to-person, etc., as the primary tool."

We want to add a word or two to this good suggestion. Great care should be exercised in cooperating with the other congregations in the area. It has always been repulsive to me and Rosemont elders to be in the "sheep stealing" business. We hope, however, that through correspondence and being close to Columbia Christian College, we can find other teammates to help in the work. Paul always worked his fields in the company of other men. We would not, therefore, be opposed to sharing the opportunities with as many as want to help in cottage work, visitation, campaigns, leading the singing and teaching. Too, it must be clearly understood that we are opposed to the "one-preacher-pulpit" philosophy on the mission field.

4. Regular schedules, especially summer sessions, should be planned to engage a number of "preacher boys" to work with the missionary on the specific field, live in his

home, learn from a man of experience what the opportunities, methods, problems and schedules of effective work are on the field. It will be "on the field" lab experience. This has proven successful with several young men with Bro. and Sis. Guild, including Rudy Wray, Sam Tumlinson, Randy Baker, Stephen Clayton, Loren Askow, Hugh Galyean, Ed Glover, Thurman Self, John Wallace and others. A couple of letters will illustrate the value of this service:

TO WHOM IT MAY CONCERN: "During the summer of 1971 our seventeen-year-old son, Stephen, spent two months in Brisbane, Australia. He had the privilege of living in the home of the Claude Guilds while there, learning first hand the joys and problems of a missionary family.

"Stephen taught scripture classes in the high schools, did personal work, preached his first sermon, led congregational singing and otherwise participated in the work and worship services, and he had the privilege of baptizing five people into Christ. He is quick to say that these months were the happiest time of his life. We consider this one of the richest experiences a young man could have.

"Stephen returned home a more mature and dedicated Christian. He was impressed with the devotion and strength of faith of the congregation there. From the time of his arrival he was greeted with love and warm hospitality. He became close to the members of the church and through his Bible classes he was able to meet and become friends with more young people.

"It is our wish that Stephen will again have an opportunity to visit and work in a mission field." SIGNED — Mr. and Mrs. Lewis Clayton, Vernon, Texas

Randy Baker expresses his thoughts about this relationship: "The purpose of this letter is to confirm my very strong belief in the advantages of coming to the mission field and working with individuals who have already established themselves in the foreign culture. Jesus established a similar precedent when he sent the apostles out two by two (Mark 6:7).

"It has been my pleasure to have worked with Claude and Sammie Guild in Brisbane, Australia, for a little over two years. As they had already had one tour of duty in Australia, their assistance in overcoming the cultural barriers was beyond value. Also, the fact that they are an older couple with vast experience has been a great asset. His example of leadership has been a great inspiration to me. Their presence has allowed my family and myself to settle into the work slower rather than having all the unfamiliar problems thrust upon us while we were trying to make the major adjustments that come from living in a strange culture.

"Truly, there is a great need on any mission field for men with great experience in the church. I do not feel there is any arrangement more beneficial than that of having an older man, with greater experience, coupled with a less experienced, younger man. The relationship that existed between Paul and the younger men, Timothy and Titus, is one that needs to be reproduced again and again in the twentieth century. I feel that my relationship with Bro. Claude has been of a similar nature and will be invaluable as far as any future service I might render in the Kingdom of God."

Rosemont and the good team of working fund-people will see great things come from these additional men who are trained on the field by the family they support and encourage.

The elders have mentioned "the primary tool" on the new field as teaching from house to house, person to person. The secret of any man's work, missionary or local, is to subscribe to the ancient principle God laid down a long time ago, "one-on-one" teaching, when God came in person and talked with Cain, Noah, Abraham, and Moses. You can't beat it. But, let me insert, local mediums of communication can be utilized to get into these homes with great effectiveness.

This personal work will be contagious and spread where all the congregation will want to be doing it. After months and years of evangelization there will be the need of a lot of personal work in edification, or keeping the saved saved and built up in the faith. There are few things as exciting as classes for new Christians. This is the time to teach them faithfulness, service, giving and forgiving.

5. Radio, Television and Newspapers: Souls are dying without Christ. We must hasten to reach them, and we have learned on the mission field the value of using radio, television, and newspaper articles effectively in the campaign for lost souls.

We learned a great lesson from Archie Waldrum. This man had the building burn around him in Alice. But he and the elders rose from the ashes and notified us that the last thing they'd cut off would be the mission program. In the midst of this tribulation, they sent a special contribution to the Indian work. Archie got outside Alice and even raised some more funds. This is another reason Tigard\Lake Oswego, Oregon, will be a success. Ministers and elders of other working-fund groups will help, such as Leonard Waggoner, Richard Pectol, J.H. Peoples, Thomas Campbell, Brother Marshall at Vernon, the minister and elders at Pueblo, Colorado, along with countless others.

7. Tools for the work: As we begin the work in Tigard\Lake Oswego we will need money for a building in which to meet. Then comes the location and purchase of land. Lastly, and more expensive, will be a building of our own. I have faith that the local work will grow and a lot of the later expense will be borne by the local brethren. Nevertheless, I am not worried about these matters. The working-fund people helped with the building in Perth and also Holland Park.

Rosemont church and the working-fund people are, as we would say in Australia, a "weird mob." Do you know that more than half of the churches and individuals support-

149

ing the work, including Rosemont, asked to have a part in this work? I will never forget the first time I went to Portland to build the work at Eastside. ROSEMONT WAS THE ONLY CHURCH THAT VOLUNTEERED TO HELP WITH THE WORK.

It is warming to know that the country church at Burkett, Texas, has been related to our work in various ways for thirty-seven years. Myra Writer and Pauline Cowles have been boosters for thirty-four years. Other personal associations have enriched our lives through the years: I baptized Sister M.L. Moore's two daughters thirty-four years ago and Sister L.V. Brooker's husband twenty-one years ago, along with her son-in-law, Lowell Goodman. Included with one of the many checks Sis. Brooker sent us through the years was a note which read, "Thank God, Brother Guild, you didn't give up until you got Daddy on board the ol' ship of Zion and he never heard a bad sermon after that."

We have had associations with Sammie's home church in Altus, Oklahoma, for thirty-four years. They supported us in Canada, helped with a building in Corvallis, Oregon, and our personal support in Yakima, Washington. We have been blessed with fellowship with Belmont in Pueblo, Colorado, for nineteen years, and their fine eldership wrote us monthly while we were in Australia. A.B. Collett was a wonderful faculty member at Columbia Christian College while I served as Vice President and Acting President for the college.

Jo Betsy Allred, widow of past governor of Texas, Jimmie Allred, asked to be on the working-fund team. She sent her check regularly and always enclosed an encouraging poem or prayer for the work. Twelve years ago, Bell Trust helped us with a building in Mount Hood, Oregon. Brother Robert Bell gave sizable checks to Ft. Worth Christian College and bought church bonds in other places we have labored. Tenth and Broad in Wichita Falls was one of the first churches to take up the Australian Challenge and

150

added to their support the full expense of the "Queensland Progress Report." We will never forget it.

Sister Effie Riddle has contributed often and she remembers when we baptized her son and daughter forty-seven years ago in Yakima, Washington. Sister B.C. Rhoten remembers when her husband was baptized at Riverside thirty-six years ago. There are too many intimate and rewarding experiences with Lawrence and Altha Richardson over the past forty years to begin to name them all: like the years he helped me with the jail services in Ft. Worth; how Bobby learned to lead singing in a young people's class and is now a capable church music man; how we wept together, with hope, at many funerals of loved ones including my daddy's.

Ned and Bettye Martin will tell you their business has never been better than since they volunteered their partnership with us in missions. Tal Campbell, former Rosemont member, came to see us, went home and got the good church at Hawthorne, California, to help us on the T.V. program.

Vernon gave one of the largest contributions to our moving expense and in a building program. They didn't know how they could carry on their mission program, but completed their building and took up additional monthly support for Sonny in Africa and us in Australia.

Linda Hurn has been like a daughter to us for many years. Lastly, when we suffered great losses in our working funds in 1969 because some churches had troubles and problems, Downtown church in Victoria picked up the balance of the loss and has become our largest monthly supporter.

Let me tell you two more things before we leave this point — most of these people have volunteered to support us because they knew our early mission endeavors when we worked with our hands and stayed on the field for as little as $75.00 a month. This support is kind of a "thank you" for the sacrificing we have done in the past. Too, when the American dollar was devalued, these working-fund people increased their funds, some several times, to help us meet contracts in Australia. (We had been having as much as 24% taken out toward the end, since the Socialist-Labor Government that dislikes America came to power.)

9. <u>Secretary:</u> Most local preachers enjoy one or more secretaries. Sis. Ruby K. Ellis, now into her second year in Australia, came to us from the Bureau of Indian Affairs in Yakima, Washington. She will go with us into our next mission. However, it is not right, when the brethren know her great talents and we have the money, not to pay this fine lady the minimum $1,800 a year salary. You will never know the load she has taken off our hands, so we can have more classes, more study and more preaching.

10. <u>Preparing and printing missionary materials</u>: A series of lessons on missionary methods should be prepared for printing, and time should be afforded the man on the field to prepare this material. An alignment with the mission departments of our Christian colleges has already demanded some of these materials and welcomes their production.

Brother Charles Hodge said, "Preachers should be encouraged to write. Again brethren misunderstand. Brethren must lift up their eyes above their local church to the brotherhood. Brethren must learn to share. . .we must cease our selfishness. The church is here to <u>serve</u> and save the world. A preacher should involve himself in community affairs. . .." I concur in what Charles has said. Some of this material will be asked for in lectureships and church-mission workshops during the weekdays, and we should give it to them. Great men like Bro. Hodge give great assistance in the specialized fields of teacher-training, church organization and youth work. Let us share our missionary know-how with others.

11. <u>Serve as well as save the area</u>: One great message the world is listening for and very rarely hears is a gospel of deeds in the community. I really believe the strength of our work in most of the places we have served has been in finding mediums of service to the community. In Holland Park it was feeding forty elderly couples a hot meal once a month and teaching Bible classes in eighteen public schools. It was putting our young people to work. We armed them with mowers, mops and brooms and sent them to clean inside and out for widows, the elderly and the sick. They enjoyed singing for shut-ins. They took orphan children to retreats, camp and their own gatherings. These kinds of activities and food, clothes, care, rent, and an over abundance of love and concern are great selling services for the gospel. Some of our working funds helped in these very things.

12. <u>Communications</u>: It was a great disappointment to our elders when we asked them to reassign us to a field closer to our home bases. We wanted to stay in Australia, but we had agreed to go to Australia for two years in the beginning and completed six. They had asked Sammie to be their sole ambassador to notify them when we had had enough, and this she did. It has broken our hearts, too, but we have given the work our strength, our hearts, our hands and there is only so much you can give and not "give in and give up," as Brother Hodge says.

It was not feasible for the elders to visit us in Australia. They bestowed their highest compliment in the six years, when we pressed them to come see the field. They said, "We have a man hired to do that work for us and it would serve little use to us as we see it, since there is no lack of confidence in our man on the field." Yet, we longed for them to witness the work of winning souls for the Savior. Many of you will get to take your holidays and visit us in Oregon. We will be strengthened and encouraged by your visits. Make plans now to take your holidays in the area.

You can catch the finest fish, pick the best berries, enjoy the finest scenery, and get a vision of reaching out to 160,000 precious souls.

13. Reaching out: I know that will happen in Tigard\Lake Oswego, Oregon. The same thing happened in Jerusalem — "They all went everywhere preaching the word." I know what happened when we lived in the Northwest the first time — 1939 through 1947. We saw men trained to preach like Clyde Teel, Willard Bradley, Jim Judd, Edward Walton and members go out to other cities. We had a part in establishing the church in Craig and Ketchikan, Alaska; McMinnville, Corvallis, Dallas, Baker, La Grande, Oregon; Walla Walla, Granger, Yakima, Richland, Washington; and Boise, Idaho. I know what has happened in Australia: Holland Park and Wynnum are radiating points to send the gospel into Norang, Toombul, Toowoomba, Southport, Gympic, Proserpine and beyond the state of Queensland. If the elders at Rosemont do not approve of this prospectus and decide that we should stay in Australia, we will just nail down our tent in this vast area and as long as the elders dictate that we stay here and sound out the word, even to the ends of the world, we, by His grace, will do it.

14. Limitations: The elders have said, "We would like to limit the time away from the area to something like four weeks per year for meetings plus a two-week vacation." I am very aware of the presence of a man in the field. Also, I would rather hold a few meetings, like Bro. Charles H. Roberson of Abilene Christian used to say, "Where others won't go."

We will build a church in Tigard\Lake Oswego and not a mission. But I hope we won't develop a dependence on the local preacher like we have in some churches in America today. If we are really honest, we have first class "pastors" in many preachers. Bro. Hodge says some very timely things: "We don't like to have you being away so much." Brethren, you mean well but misunderstand. A congregation should not want a preacher others would not have! Brethren should feel pride in knowing their preacher is wanted and needed. Brethren are selfish. Why not share? Why not rejoice when your preacher serves the brotherhood? To stay, a preacher must be allowed to 'get away.' You get 'bogged down' at home. . . .Invitations to preach are 'ego-messages.'" The elders at Rosemont know that a preacher's schedule cannot be "crystalized" but must be "plastic." Therefore, we will submit to their will and wishes in this vital matter of staying close to the work.

15. <u>Systematic Approach</u>: The elders have suggested, "We would like to see a planned systematic approach to evangelizing this metropolitan area: section by section, block by block. This could involve people to come in and canvass an area and others to come in behind them and follow up in assisting in this evangelizing."

The elders are wise in this evaluation. We cannot afford to miss a soul. Columbia Christian College has added another year of college work in Biblical studies. They are honoring and accepting Bible credits transferred from some of the preachers' training schools. Won't it be wonderful to use some of these men and women who are in this great college? The students do attend most all the congregations in Portland, and it is reasonable to believe they will be there helping as well. There will be other campaigns, as we have mentioned earlier, that will cover the area.

16. <u>Partnership is vital</u>: Last but not least, there isn't any question about it, all your prayers have been felt, helpful and answered many, many times. We have the finest partners in the Lord and his dear Father, and they will continue to abide with us as long as we are faithful. Let us never leave God out of our plans just because we are finding new life in a new area closer to home. "I will never leave thee." "Lo, I am with you always." Amen

Chapter 12

THE TIGARD TRIUMPH

Our hearts swelled with great emotions as we crossed the Cascade Mountains and on the western slopes of Mount Hood saw the lights of the greater Portland, Lake Oswego, Tigard and Beaverton areas. There were one million people waiting to hear the gospel, especially in the Tigard area, for the first time. We were filled with pride to think that the Rosemont eldership with whom we had worked for fourteen years had surveyed the field and made the decision to send us to Tigard. We had the same working fund team we had in Australia, and God would begin opening doors the next day in a totally new field.

Personnel made a well-rounded team. Woodrow W. Hughes, a personal yoke-fellow for forty-eight years, missionary and minister, was asked to go with us and head up visitation and the educational work. (Two years before the elders alerted us about the possibilities in the immediate area, Bro. Hughes had written us in Australia that he saw great possibilities there and wanted to interest us.) He and Gracie were ready and just the right couple. He had published his own cottage class materials and was a specialist in his field. He was self-employed and later took support for this work from the church in Hereford, Texas.

La Vega Parker and Nancy had just completed a tour of duty in the Caribbean. Nancy was a niece to one of the Rosemont elders, James Knott. Support was found for the Parkers, and he would be another experienced team member and excellent song leader. Ruby K. Ellis also came to us from Australia as the church secretary.

Finding a place to meet: The Oregon-Washington churches had just run a T.V. program on channel 12, "Impact for Christ." J.T. Bristow directed the program. It ran five nights, and there were 742 responses to the program. Glenn and Cindy Elliott responded for material from Tigard. They lived next door to the I.O.O.F. Hall we were going to contract for meetings. When we approached them, Glenn came to the door, and I could see his wife in the living room reading her Bible. I immediately asked him why she was reading the Bible, and he related how they moved to Oregon from Clebourne, Texas. He explained that they were Baptists and unhappy about their spiritual welfare and decided to just get the Bible down and read their way into a better relationship with God. (This was a 20th century opportunity like the eunuch in Acts, chapter eight.) Classes were begun immediately, and they obeyed the gospel before we rented the hall. Glenn said, "I want to go to work. Please give me something to do." We rented the hall next door, gave him the keys and said, "Glenn, you are our door-and-key man."

A date is set. June 17, 1973, was selected as opening day. The rent was $50.00 a week. We placed a nice ad in the newspaper with a news story of the church having a beginning and immediately we began finding people. The Simmerson family had lived in the area six years. They were from Waco, Texas, and unfaithful to their Lord. They came and were restored. Harry and Jo Hix were reclaimed, and Sister Strickland from Zepher, Texas, was restored after seventeen years of unfaithfulness. Other families wanted their children to have the experience of starting with a new work and they came to us. Keith and Dora Ann Dodson, Bill and Mary Ellen Allen, Jerry and Ann Milstead, and Tommie and Maudie Thomas. Sister Jennings of Hereford, Texas, whose brother, Alvin Jennings, was a missionary, was enthusiastic about our mission effort. Her son, Duke, had been in the Air Force in Japan and was being discharged. She wanted me to contact him and encourage him to move to Tigard and set up his medical practice there. We did, and Duke and Becky Jennings came and joined us with great zeal and excitement.

An invitation was sent to each congregation in the area about our opening and unbeknown to us, Dr. Rex Johnston, President of Columbia Christian College, wrote each church to send two families for six months to help us get started. Woodrow, La Vega and I had hit a snag. I had a letter from a fine preacher in India — Bontha Ramson of Chennupalli, India — that he was walking each weekend to fill his appointments and needed a bicycle. We laid all of this before the Lord and said, "Lord, the bicycle will come first. After the bicycle, rent will come next." We liked this because missions had first priority in our first collection. God heard and understood our desires. The day came and 171 people signed the register. We had people there from twenty-five sister congregations, four states and a special blessing with J.P. Sanders speaking on, "The Purpose of the Church." The offering was taken and we collected $475.00. Praise the Lord, we had money for a bicycle for Bro. Ramson and funds for rent for several months.

A pretty little sister-in-law of Cindy Elliott was asked to put the bulletins out — Pam Elliott. She had attended classes too. We passed out slips to all who wanted to place membership, be baptized or restored and when the slips came in, Pan expressed a desire to obey the gospel. We told her, "Pam, put the bulletins down, come up here and make the good confession."

Some of the communities represented for the opening day were Beaverton, Corvallis, Sweet Home, Monmouth, Newberg, Prineville, Redmond, Hood River, Sherwood, Oregon City, Klamath Falls, Eugene, Springfield, Molalla, Woodburn, Oregon; Yakima, Vancouver, Pasco,

Tacoma, Washington; Ft. Worth, Texas; and in Portland the Central, Eastside, Mallory, and Linwood congregations.

Newcomers service contracted: As soon as we moved into our home, a nicely dressed lady came to the door representing various businesses through the agency, Newcomer Services. She wore an apron with pockets full of literature. She gave us a coupon to get a suit cleaned at a cleaning establishment, another for a pound of bacon at Safeway and many, many more. We learned there were ten women working west of the Willamette River and in our area they would visit one thousand homes a month. It appeared to me, they would represent our cause very well with a nice brochure about the church and free classes to any newcomers to Portland, Tigard, and Lake Oswego. The next day I went to their office, approached the manager, and he was very harsh and ugly. "I have managed this office twenty-eight years, and I have never had a church represented, because they all want money and have nothing to give people." "Wait a minute," I said, "I'll show you one that has something to give people." I ran to the car, brought up the Jule Miller slides and showed him five nicely printed commentaries on the slide presentation that would be given to everyone that finished the course. When I told him the commentaries were worth $7.50 and would be offered at no cost, he was stunned. He wanted to know where the films would be shown. We related that the choice was with the viewers — their home, our home, or our hall. After some thought he said, "Do you have $150.00?" That was the initial charge, and there would be a monthly charge of seventy-five dollars. They would give us a pull sheet on the homes visited, and it would include the names of all the family members, ages, business association, religious affiliation and much more. We printed 10,000 brochures for the girls to use and began having immediate results. Bro. Hughes was running day and night with classes, and the prospects and open doors were so great we had to discontinue our association with the Newcomer Service after one year.

In addition to the converts, other families saw the advantage of a new work and came to join us: David and Donna Treat, Don and Joetta Harikian, Vern and Judy Bissell, Harvey and Edie Clark, and Monfred and Lois Alexander.

A strange request is lodged. We had a letter from Grant Houser, Director of the Bible Chair in Tahlequah, Oklahoma. He related how he had gone to Reed College in Portland. He had enjoyed seeing them drag the cross across the soccer field when they played Columbia Christian College and was proud to be a first-class hippie. But, students from Columbia went to Reed to work the campus for Christ. Some of them got to him, and he obeyed the gospel. He went on to Harding College and became the director of a Bible chair for the churches of Christ. His mother lived in Portland. He wanted to visit her and try to reach her soul by inviting her to hear him preach a sermon. He doubted that any church of Christ that remembered him would let him preach from their pulpits, so he contacted us. Since we were new, he hoped we would honor his request. We invited Grant to preach for us. He brought his mother, Helen Cole, and I saw a man that night empty his soul for Christ's sake to reach the heart of his mother. It was a great night, and Helen obeyed the gospel. By this time Ruby K. Ellis had to go to Montana to be with her daughter, and Helen was retiring as secretary to a steel company in Portland. She was one of the old-fashioned secretaries that could take dictation and spell. We employed her immediately, and she was a great asset to our work. Grant Houser was exceedingly happy, Helen was happy, and we were all very happy.

A year passed and God was blessing our work and the I.O.O.F. hall was filled. In fact, we had classes in the lobbies, the rest rooms and the furnace room. It was time to look for a home of our own. Woodrow Hughes was in the real estate business, and he found five acres in the Summerfield addition close to Tigard High School. The property had beautiful trees and a little house and garage. An elderly couple owned it and did not want to see the property go into a housing development but wanted the land to remain open and beautiful. When we told them we wanted it for a church, they were happy. They were so excited about it, they we were willing to reduce the asking price of $40,000 by ten percent. We bought it for $36,000. It would take an additional $17,500 to bring the sewer and water to the property. We made an appeal to our friends who had supported us over forty-five years of mission work, and the $53,500 came in a three-month period.

Building becomes a problem and opportunity. Building costs were climbing, and we couldn't construct a building for less than $400,000. What would this young church do for a home of its own? Again, Woodrow Hughes was in the right place at the right time. He learned that the oldest frame church building in Tigard would be for sale for $75,000 and with some remodeling could meet our needs until our new building could be built. The congregation agreed to go for it. Special contributions were taken, funds raised, and we were in our new home.

We were looking for a new architect. Our special friend in Dallas, Linda Hurn, went to church at Preston Road and knew an architect there, Aubrey Hallum. She shared our needs with him, and he was planning a trip to Portland. While in Portland, he visited us. We discussed building plans and came to the conclusion that we needed a building that would make people feel free to enter. We did not want it to look like a church with stained glass and other such trappings. From out in left field I suggested we build it to look like a savings and loan building. After all, we were going to be in the saving business. We also wanted a drive-through carport arrangement, which would be nice in rainy weather.

162

Bro. Hallum excitedly said, "I have been wanting to do something like this for a church all my professional life, and my services will be free to a church that is willing to do something different from a so-called 'Paden-plan building!'" The church immediately began making plans for a new property.

Missions were on our mind. Many opportunities presented themselves for this young church to do missionary work. Everyone was in the mood to help because we believed the more we did for others the more the Lord would do for us. Dr. Duke Jennings, M.D., and Bob McKee, attorney, lived in the area of Scappoose, Oregon, twenty-five miles from Tigard. A Baptist building with seating for two hundred, ten classrooms and office space became available for $26,000. Jennings and McKee signed a note for the property, and brethren from the Peninsula congregation in Portland became interested. Funds were gathered in Portland, Tigard and from distant places, and we had started another congregation of the Lord's church in the area. We were asked to help in their first revival meeting and one person was baptized. Tigard men filled the pulpit and in August, 1977, Jimmie Hughes from Chickasaw, Oklahoma, came to work with them.

Missions for overseas attracted the attention of the Tigard church. Bill and Margie Wells of Hood River, Oregon, accompanied Sammie and me on a world tour of missions. We visited the Holy Land, Kenya, India, Australia and New Zealand. That 1977 tour was fruitful. There were two hundred fifteen baptisms on the trip, and Tigard was invited to have a part in the ministries of some great men, especially in India.

We accepted the oversight of M. John Balasundarum in Vijayawada, M.G. Parkasam in Komerapudi, and P. Balaraju in Chilakaluripet. We provided partial support of Bontha Ramson in Chennupalli, Sonny Guild in Kenya and Jimmie Hughes in Scappoose. At the close of 1978 we called for a roll call of additions at home and abroad. (We had set a goal of 1,000 additions for the year.) Sonny reported 277; Bontha Ramson, 99; M. John Balasundaram, 352; P. Balaraju, 237; M.G. Prakasam, 63; Jimmie Hughes, 16; and Tigard, 48. It was a year of great harvest with 1,092 souls, and everyone was working.

Early in 1976 building plans were completed, and it called for $50,000 cash and an outlay of church bonds for $250,000. By this time our membership had grown to over two hundred. It was very exciting to see members of this congregation buy $100,000 worth of bonds. In fact, sixty-six families in Oregon bought bonds and fifty-nine families out of the state of Oregon purchased them.

While the construction was underway, Tigard church had an offer to sell the old building we had remodelled. We paid $75,000 for it, and the Lord came through with an offer of $100,000. It served us well for three years. The extra funds went into the new property. The dedication came September 18, 1977, with a lectureship. Lynn Rhodes of Wichita Falls; Archie Waldrum from Alice, Texas; M. Norvel Young, Chancellor of Pepperdine University; and Dr. J.P. Sanders, President of Columbia Christian College were the speakers. Honorable mention was made of the builder, E. Lee Robinson, architect Aubrey Hallum and all the bond-holders.

Seven years in Tigard saw it grow from two families to the second largest church in Oregon. The brethren have added on to the property. They hired Sonny Guild as their evangelist, who has been with them ten years. They have eight elders, including Gordon Teel, who shares the pulpit with Sonny, and they have twenty-one deacons. They are still involved heavily in missionary work.

164

A Call To Springtown, Texas

After forty-five years of preaching with twenty-eight of them in mission fields, Sammie and I talked about one more experience like the one at Riverside in Ft. Worth. We enjoyed the eldership there and the properties for preaching and classes. (They had an expansive pulpit with room to do a lot of illustrated sermons.) Tigard had become self-supporting, and Sonny was located with them as their pulpit minister. We were ready for a non-missionary experience and shared our desires with the Lord.

In the spring of 1980 I was invited to speak at the Ft. Worth lectures. Representatives from Springtown, Texas, heard me and invited me to speak there on a Wednesday night. The building had the same large pulpit, and there were about four hundred members. (Springtown is a town of eighteen hundred people.) The eldership was mature and just wonderful. They liked to do missionary work and also had the oversight of Chimala Mission Hospital in Tanzania, E. Africa.

June 1, 1980, we sold our home in Tigard and moved into a nice parsonage and went to work with the Springtown church. David Cotham was the youth minister and an excellent preacher. The church had helped us before with contributions to our various fields of labor. Foy Lowe, Glenn Cooper, Dwight Pyle and Alex Thomas were the elders. The church had an imposing impact on the city. The superintendent of schools, chief of police, mayor, and editor of the paper were members. Every project in the city involved members of the church.

One of the joys of this pulpit was the responses that came with nearly every service. Also, Springtown was close enough to Ft. Worth, where we enjoyed the company of former friends. In addition, the elders enlisted my services immediately to help with fund raising for the Chimala Mission Hospital. The hospital had a campus of three hundred fifty acres, a sixty-six-bed hospital, housing for most of its staff and woodworking and metal shops. During our stay at Springtown they added a maternal health center and a duplex for staff. Our involvement included getting churches to send boxes of bandages, gowns, plastic bottles, blankets and personal things to the missionaries. We have averaged more than four hundred boxes a year. People were responsive to our needs and at one time we had a surplus of $100,000. Those days are over, and they now operate on a $205,000 budget.

Springtown church alerted us about the fast lane, the fatigue and frustration that comes from the mission fields. The call from Springtown helped us rebuild our physical, spiritual and emotional abilities. 1983 came, and I could draw my social security along with Sammie. We drew it when I was sixty-seven and launched into a program that would work with our social security income.

It had always been my desire to "do the work of an evangelist." Churches have been generous, calling on my services in gospel or revival meetings. A local work is seven days a week and more hours per day than I want to talk about. Demands are made beyond the pulpit to jobs of administrating, fund raising, counseling, clowning with the children and being a first class bell-hop for the church. In June, 1983, we resigned at Springtown and laid plans to move to Portland, Oregon. We wanted to answer more meeting calls, be a supply preacher in the Portland area and work for Columbia Christian College as special assistant to the President. The Springtown elders wanted us to continue with fund raising for the Chimala Hospital. Portland was also chosen because seven of our nine grandchildren were there. Sammie and I moved to Portland, where we are now serving the Lord with great joy and fulfillment in returning to the great Northwest where our ministry began.

166

Chapter 13

MY MISSION:
WORLD-WIDE EVANGELISM

My calls for gospel meetings took me to every continent but South America. Germany called us for several meetings. Singapore with Gordon Hogan and Ten Can Koon and his wife, Baby Koon, were rich experiences. We had two campaigns in Seremban, Malaysia. Colombo Sri Lanka was very exciting. We made a number of campaigns in Africa, namely to Kenya and Tanzania.

Over a period of nineteen years we made nine trips to India, where we had the privilege of baptizing thousands of souls into Christ. It was a great thrill to take three of my grandsons, Jon Love, Chris Guild and Hugh Galyean, on two of those trips. They preached with me and spent many hours in the rivers of India baptizing people who had come confessing Jesus as their Lord. We established the church in a number of cities in India, and at Enkole we immersed two hundred thirty-eight people, the largest day for numbers in my fifty-five years of preaching. We helped start the church in Chennupalli, Komerapudi, Pedambadipudi and Narasaraopet. At this time we are responsible for the support of fifteen native preachers in India, and they are doing great things for the Lord.

While I have travelled to so many countries and all over the United States to preach the gospel, it has been particularly satisfying to return to my beginnings. At the age of seventy-four, my mission and my commitment to evangelism in virgin fields continue. I have accepted a new missionary challenge in the great Northwest. The Spring-town church, that has been so faithful to support and encourage us in many of our missionary endeavors, has agreed to support us in our newest undertaking for God. Sammie and I have agreed to work with a small congregation in Gladstone, Oregon. They have hired a fine young man from Columbia Christian College to serve as their pulpit minister. He has a great name for a gospel preacher — Thomas Nelson. Sammie and I will teach classes, support and encourage Thomas in his work, and help this church take root and grow. What a blessing it is to help establish and develop the church in another city in the state of Oregon.

Returning to the Northwest has also allowed us to renew our active involvement with Columbia Christian College and to see first hand the great progress the college has made in recent years. Over the past five years I have worked as a special assistant to the President of Columbia, Dr. Gary Elliott. I have served on the Board of Trustees and participated in several fund raising efforts. It is good to see the fruits of our labors with Columbia as we visit churches and see great and effective leaders who were educated and prepared for service in the Kingdom at Columbia Christian College.

We have also been able to enjoy the love of our children, grandchildren, and great-grandchildren, all of whom live in the Portland area except D'Esta's family. They have lavished their love upon us, and this is the way it ought to be. As we conclude these pages it is nice to know that all of our children and their mates are deeply involved in the work of the church. All nine of our grandchildren have obeyed the gospel.

As I reflect on the mission to which I dedicated myself as a young man on a farm in Idaho and the ensuing years which have taken Sammie and me on a great adventure of faith, I think of the words inscribed on a placque that hangs

168

on my office wall. It was presented to Sammie and me at the 1989 Pepperdine University Lectures in recognition for a lifetime of Christian service. It reads:

PEPPERDINE UNIVERSITY

Distinguished Christian Service Award

in honor of
Claude A. and Sammie Guild
Devoted servants of Christ, Enthusiastic workers in the church,
Beloved Missionaries in the Great Northwest,
Generous supporters of Columbia Christian College,
and ones who have given their lives
to the cause for which Christ died.

Presented on
April 20, 1989
at the
46th Annual Bible Lectureship

My advice to young preachers today is never look back. Leave your lives hidden in Jesus Christ, and he will chart a great course for you.